MONETARISM
and
MACRO-ECONOMICS

IEA F

MONETARISM
and
MACRO-ECONOMICS

Contributions on the current policy debate in the UK

DAVID K. H. BEGG □ R. A. BATCHELOR
RICHARD JACKMAN and RICHARD LAYARD
MICHAEL BEENSTOCK and PATRICK MINFORD

With Commentaries by
Alan Budd · David Currie · C. A. E. Goodhart
Harold Rose · D. A. Peel · Samuel Brittan
Jon Shields

Edited and Introduced by PATRICK MINFORD

Published by
The Institute of Economic Affairs
1987

First published in November 1987 by
THE INSTITUTE OF ECONOMIC AFFAIRS
© The Institute of Economic Affairs 1987

ISSN 0305-814X
ISBN 0-255 36203-X

Typeset, printed and bound in England by
Latimer Trend & Company Ltd, Plymouth

Contents

Preface

In organising this conference and editing its proceedings for the IEA, I have relied on the IEA's staff for the difficult parts: writing to everyone, arranging the venue, resolving practical difficulties, and so on. I thank in particular Eve Pollecoff and Ken Smith. Ralph Harris chivvied us all along and kept us to our pre-arranged timetable. Martin Anderson went carefully through the manuscripts and made numerous useful suggestions for clarification and stylistic improvement. Michael Solly copy-edited the manuscript as capably as always. Our thanks, too, go to RTZ for generously making available to us their splendid conference and catering facilities.

The day's proceedings were chaired firmly and fairly by Geoffrey Maynard; I am most grateful to him for undertaking this arduous task. At the risk of gilding the lily, I have added an introduction to assist those who may well be confused by the profusions of the debate, to whet the reader's appetite for the main papers and events, and to satisfy my own desire to find unifying themes. It is a personal account rather than an attempt at dispassionate summary which, though less provocative, would also, I decided, be less interesting.

This book of *Readings* contains a minimum of technical argument. Where technicalities have had to remain, they have been hived off into special sections or appendices for easier reading.

October 1987   P.M.

Introduction

PATRICK MINFORD
University of Liverpool

The Author

A. P. L. (PATRICK) MINFORD has been Edward Gonner Professor of Applied Economics, University of Liverpool, since 1976. Formerly Visiting Hallsworth Research Fellow, University of Manchester, 1974–75. Sometime Consultant to the Ministry of Overseas Development, Ministry of Finance (Malawi), Courtaulds, Treasury, British Embassy (Washington). Editor of *National Institute Economic Review*, 1975–76.

He is the author of *Substitution Effects, Speculation and Exchange Rate Stability* (1978), and of essays published in *Inflation in Open Economies* (1976); *The Effects of Exchange Adjustments* (1977); *On How to Cope with Britain's Trade Position* (1977); *Contemporary Economic Analysis* (1978); co-author of *Unemployment: Cause and Cure* (1983, 2nd edn. 1985). He contributed papers to two IEA Seminars: 'Macro-economic Controls on Government', in *The Taming of Government* (IEA Readings 21, 1979), and 'Monetarism, Inflation and Economic Policy', in *Is Monetarism Enough?* (IEA Readings 24, 1980). He also contributed 'Restore Market Momentum and Fight On' to *Could Do Better* (Occasional Paper 62, 1982), and 'From Macro to Micro via Rational Expectations' to *The Unfinished Agenda* (1986); and he was joint author (with Michael Peel and Paul Ashton) of *The Housing Morass* (Hobart Paperback No. 25, IEA, 1987).

To the one-day seminar on which this *Readings* is based, the IEA invited a number of experts concerned with the debate on economic policy in Britain to discuss the major macro-economic issues of the day. Essentially, the morning debate was devoted to inflation, and specifically the roles of fiscal and monetary policy in containing it with the minimum of adverse consequences. The afternoon debate was devoted to unemployment; the focus for policy was on whether a variety of 'special measures', reflation, or a return to competition in the labour market were, singly or in coalition, appropriate cures.

1. The Role of Fiscal Policy and the MTFS

In the first paper of the morning, Professor David Begg, of Birkbeck College, London, discussed the role of fiscal policy and the concept of the 'Medium-Term Financial Strategy' (MTFS) in which the Conservative Government has set five-year rolling targets for public-sector borrowing and growth in the supply of money. Begg charts the decline of demand-management as a motivation of fiscal policy in the UK; Mrs Margaret Thatcher's Government *reduced* the deficit in 1981/82 at the trough of the business cycle. Indeed, throughout the first half of the 1980s fiscal policy has been restrictive on any measure (Begg discusses various 'adjusted' measures). This attitude of the Government infuriated its Keynesian critics; and Begg goes on to provide a rationale for it as a counter-inflationary strategy.

His point can be put very simply. If inflation is being controlled by fixing monetary targets, the government's deficit will add to its debt. But if this debt grows too rapidly, it threatens to undermine confidence in the government's published monetary targets: the public may fear that, because government is unwilling to put up taxes, it will be tempted to inflate faster (by printing more money) in order to reduce the real burden of debt interest or worse—it might even default. In an open economy, 'the public' includes many foreigners who may be especially sensitive about these problems, having no direct control over the matter. The MTFS is an attempt, albeit a crude one (perhaps necessarily so in the rough-and-ready world of democratic politics), to limit the growth of government debt so that this threat does not emerge.

In recent years much attention has been devoted by researchers to the conditions under which this threat *could* emerge. It has to be admitted frankly that we do not understand them very well: what we have is a variety of models in which fears for loss of reputation may restrain a government from inflationary default on its debts; alternatively, a government may bind itself by some mechanism (such as conditions imposed by the International Monetary Fund) penalising it in the event of such policies. But it is not yet clear how strong these restraints can be made. What common sense tells us, at any rate, is that 'credibility' is a fragile and precious commodity for those who control monetary conditions, and that British governments have been painfully short of it at least until the 1980s. Begg notes that the markets believed, rightly or wrongly, in the real possibility of default by the British government on its debt (whether open or by rekindling inflation) and were as a result sensitive to the level of government debt; he agrees that the Government therefore had no choice but to follow stern policies on the debt.

However, Begg also examines long-term projections of expenditure, revenue and debt interest (summarised in the 'permanent' deficit of the state sector), and concludes that in practice British government finances have been in extremely good shape, not only in the 1980s but, more controversially, in the mid-1970s. In qualification of this conclusion, the good performance in the mid-1970s arose from the high inflation which much reduced the value of outstanding government debt, and in so doing realised the very fears public finance policy should be designed to allay; it can, therefore, hardly be considered a triumph. Begg notes, furthermore, that by 1984 a 'permanent' deficit had finally emerged because the Government was spending its oil and gas revenues, which would dwindle (all too quickly, as it turned out, when oil prices fell rapidly in 1986). The conclusion seems to be that *now* it is right that the Government should exercise caution in its finances if it is not to be forced to raise taxes later. As for the past, fiscal policy has, Begg argues, at least succeeded in restoring financial confidence.

Begg examines two other aspects of fiscal policy: its direct role as a counter-inflationary instrument, and its indirect role in strengthening the supply side by changing the rules of government intervention. He argues that both have been important. Fiscal policy has, he thinks, been used directly against inflation; a nominal public sector borrowing requirement (PSBR) target with an index-linked tax system will deflate the economy automatically as inflation rises (he has in mind especially the effect of rising interest rates on debt interest; spending programmes are then squeezed). The rules of intervention, too, have been changed to become 'non-accommodative'; if the PSBR is fixed, then, when industries or state sector programmes are 'in trouble', there can be no 'quick fix' by borrowing. Instead, unpopular taxes must be raised; and this, Begg argues, creates a new pressure for efficiency among economic sectors previously accustomed to easy government help.

Begg concludes that, although the generally tough fiscal policy of the 1980s has undeniably caused losses in output, and although we have yet to see these losses unequivocally recouped by improved supply-side performance, fiscal policy has nevertheless played an important part in bringing and keeping down inflation, and its supply-side aspect may well bring significant long-term gains.

* * *

Discussion ranged widely over the issues raised by this opening paper. Professor Alan Budd, of the London Business School, argued that the role of fiscal policy in backing up the credibility of monetary targets was best fulfilled by stating PSBR targets in nominal terms; then, if inflation was stimulated by monetary expansion, real government spending would automatically have to contract, creating pressure on the government to reduce monetary expansion. In contrast, targeting the 'real PSBR' would protect or even enhance real government spending in these circumstances; this effect was illustrated in the mid-1970s when the real PSBR was small or even in surplus, largely because high inflation was reducing the real cost of debt interest, thus permitting both government spending to increase and real debt to fall relatively to GNP.

This approach was supported by Professor Michael Beenstock and others from the floor. They noted that a long-run nominal PSBR target effectively restricted the possible growth of money in the long term because in the long term people will want a constant proportion of government bonds and money in their portfolios; with the PSBR determining the growth rate of total government liabilities (money and bonds), this must also be the growth rate of money. Thus the PSBR target would act as a further guarantee of monetary credibility. Against this view, Professor Charles Good-hart and others argued that the possibility of the government raising foreign debt destroyed this link; but it was pointed out that there was an automatic limit on foreign debt placed by the capacity to service debt and by rising risk premiums. This discussion usefully extended Begg's analysis of credibility, although, of course, it still cannot answer the question of why the PSBR limits should themselves be credible.

Professor David Currie, of Queen Mary College, London, focussed on the 'game theory' aspects of Begg's paper. Had the rules of intervention ('the game') really changed for the better under Mrs Thatcher, he asked? He and some others on the floor (including Henry Neuberger, economic adviser to Mr Neil Kinnock, and Andrew Britton, the director of the National Institute of Economic and Social Research), while conceding that the Government had established a useful 'threat strategy' against inflationary behaviour by the private sector, felt that it could be much more flexible and subtle in its strategy. For example, it could offer 'reflation' in return for wage restraint, while keeping its threat in reserve if this deal broke down. Such a deal would require corporatism—co-operation between major 'social partners' represented by the TUC, the CBI and the Government. This 'co-operative strategy' would be an improvement on the existing 'non-co-operative' rules of the game, where the Government declares its fixed monetary framework and then lets unions, workers and firms do the best they can for themselves within it.

Not surprisingly, perhaps, these ideas for a revival of demand-management and incomes policy under a different name aroused some scepticism on the floor in the light of the repeated and failed British experiments with such policies since the Second World War. Given general agreement, however, that, to control inflation, a monetary and fiscal framework (at least) is necessary, the only potential role left for incomes policy would be to reduce the rate of unemployment and thus have a beneficial 'micro' effect on the operation of individual labour markets. This topic was discussed in the afternoon (below). As for demand-management, there seemed also to be some agreement that its role would at best be limited in the absence of an incomes policy (or equivalent measures) effective in this way. Thus it seems that any 'improvement' on Mrs Thatcher's 'hands-off' fiscal and monetary framework would at least be contingent on progress in reducing unemployment.

2. Monetary Indicators and Operating Targets

In the morning session, Mr Roy Batchelor turned to the issue of *how* money should be controlled, it being assumed that some framework of monetary discipline is necessary for the control of inflation. Batchelor first discusses possible *indicators* of monetary trends and, second, possible operating procedures for short-term policy; the two questions, as he emphasises, are quite separate.

An indicator of monetary trends will be used as a target for monetary policy over the longer term. It should therefore have a strong relationship with inflation; and this relationship should be clearly understood, so that if people believe the authorities will adhere to this target, it will influence their expectations of inflation. Anchoring expectations will reduce the volatility of inflation in response to shocks.

Batchelor reviews the Thatcher Government's experience with the monetary indicators it has chosen as targets. The behaviour of £M3 has been, he concludes, wayward and misleading; it was a targeting disaster essentially because of changes since 1979 in financial markets (the abolition of exchange controls and the 'corset' tax on deposit expansion, more competition, and so on). Its relationship with inflation broke down after 1979, although before that statistical studies had ranked it above other monetary aggregates as an inflation predictor. M0, the monetary base (consisting of currency in circulation and bank reserves), has performed better since 1979, he suggests, because it has been least affected by the competition to pay interest on other forms of 'money'. Batchelor argues for a measure of money which weights all types of assets according to their probability of use in transactions; but he concedes that in practice this weighting device is unlikely to satisfy the need he identified for public understanding, and so the best bet for the time being is M0.

Money GDP and the exchange rate have also been suggested as indicators. Batchelor points out that the growth of money GDP is essentially identical with inflation over the long term (when real growth should average out at its trend rate), and it is therefore not suitable as an indicator of (future) inflation. The exchange rate reflects both inflation and real shocks (such as changes in the price of oil or in productivity at home or abroad), current and anticipated; so that while it may signal future inflation, it may equally well signal events quite extraneous to the control of inflation.

Batchelor turns next to operating procedures. Essentially there are three possibilities: (i) the targeting of interest rates; (ii) control of the monetary base; or (iii) the targeting of exchange rates (as in the EMS). Each implies a different pattern of (essentially financial) uncertainty. The first, he argues, will give less uncertainty in interest rates but more in the supply of money (inflation); the second gives the opposite; the third reduces uncertainty about exchange rates at the expense of increased uncertainty about interest rates and inflation. The issue then becomes one of determining the best 'trade-off' between these methods. Batchelor considers the present procedure of targeting the monetary base (whereby interest rates are adjusted from time to time to keep M0 within a short-term target range) a reasonable compromise between uncertainty about interest rates and inflation. But he regards exchange-rate uncertainty as a much lesser evil than these twin uncertainties, because those vulnerable to it (such as export firms) can protect themselves through the forward markets whereas ordinary individuals cannot easily protect themselves against inflation or interest-rate volatility.

* * *

Batchelor's paper provoked both Goodhart and Professor Harold Rose into attacks on its 'over-simple' monetarist model of the economy. To this Batchelor replied that he was unclear in what material respects for the issues he was examining it should be complicated; a model is after all (like all analysis) a *deliberate* abstraction designed to focus on factors of vital quantitative significance. 'Sticky prices' in goods markets were suggested; but add these and money trends still determine inflation trends, while the trade-offs Batchelor identifies are if anything exacerbated (for example, sticky prices give you *more* exchange-rate volatility under floating rates).

On the issue of indicators, several people, including Rose and Mr Samuel Brittan, felt despondent about identifying any good *money* indicator of inflation in present conditions of competitive banking. This deficiency made them sympathetic in varying degrees to the exchange rate as such an indicator, provided it was purged by intelligent judgement of the effects of real shocks; the EMS now seemed attractive on these grounds. Brittan also argued that growth in money GDP should not be regarded merely as equal to inflation plus a trend; while this might be true in the very long run, in the short and even medium term growth in money GDP could move well ahead of inflation because of lags in the transmission mechanism (the 'Phillips curve') from demand to inflation. So it was a useful indicator, even if it had the disadvantage of being published with some delay.

Others argued that, given the rather modest lead of money GDP on inflation (at times no lead at all—*cf.* Batchelor's Chart on p. 70), this information delay made it of little practical use. One might as well target inflation itself and be done with it. (To which Brittan would no doubt reply that this prevents monetary policy from responding to a recession in conditions of low inflation; but for discussion of such demand-management issues, above, p. 6.) As for the exchange rate, such controversy attaches to determining the appropriate 'real' exchange rate at any time—with little consensus among professional market men, let alone economists—that 'purging out' real shocks is fraught with practical difficulty.

Operating procedures?

What then of operating procedures? Again there was a strong lobby, from more or less the same voices, for the exchange rate in the role of control mechanism. Goodhart suggested that forward markets were too short term to protect firms against exchange-rate uncertainty; but, since forward cover can be purchased for *any* maturity desired (banks providing it beyond the usual maturities simply quote the relevant maturity's interest differential), this suggestion seems unfounded. Any firm concerned to 'lock in' today's exchange rate (adjusted for interest arbitrage) can do so at trivial cost. The same seems not so true of individuals facing uncertainty about interest rates or inflation, although markets for hedging against this uncertainty have developed in the wake of the turmoil of the 1970s (we have mortgage interest linked to base rate, indexed bonds, wages re-negotiated annually, if not more frequently, through 'wage drift', and so on). What all this suggests is that the trade-offs between different types of uncertainty shift as government changes its priorities; presumably in the end, *whatever* quantity government chooses to stabilise, people will protect themselves against risks in the manner they prefer and neutralise the impact of government on their risks. Yet it seems valid to focus on what the *current* trade-off is and for government to adapt itself to

9

that, because it is presumably costly for us all to change our habits as government changes its mind. This is Batchelor's approach, and it does argue in favour of sticking with current monetary control procedures, if only because we have now learnt to live with them.

3. A Programme to Reduce the 'Natural' Rate of Unemployment

The afternoon session on unemployment began with a paper by Mr Richard Jackman and Professor Richard Layard, who suggested a programme of measures designed to bring down the 'natural' rate of unemployment (that is, the rate at which the economy would settle in the long run) and simultaneously to close what they perceived as the gap between the actual and natural rates of unemployment.

Jackman and Layard focus on the special position of the long-term unemployed who are, they argue, exerting no downward pressure on real wages; consequently, if drawn into employment by special schemes, they would not exert upward pressure either. They propose an extension of the Community Programme to give those unemployed for more than a year a job guarantee. This should be financed by borrowing; but the cost would be low because the government would pay out less under the programme than it now does in benefits. This modest-cost 'targeted reflation' would thus create extra jobs for the long-term unemployed without reducing existing jobs, because real wages would be unaffected.

They wish to go further, however, and put *downward* pressure on real-wage demands among those currently employed; for this purpose they propose a Tax-Based Incomes Policy (TIP). They reject administratively-based incomes policy of the usual sort on the grounds of inflexibility; such inflexibility is the cause, they believe, of the eventual breakdown of these traditional policies. TIP they envisage as a permanent change in the tax structure, which would penalise high wage settlements without outlawing them. They propose a norm for wage increases for firms with over 100 employees; these firms would be assessed for the tax on their PAYE wages bill divided by the number of their employees. If their 'wage increase', so defined, exceeded the norm, the excess would attract TIP at some penal rate; 100 per cent has been suggested by Layard and Professor Steven Nickell in an Employment Institute publication.[1] Any revenue raised from TIP would be returned to the corporate sector by a general deduction from National Insurance contributions, so that corporate profitability in total would not suffer.

A 'gateway' for profit-related pay is proposed (*cf.* Nickell and Layard, *op. cit.*) to permit 'genuine' increases in productivity; to avoid window-dressing wages as profits, a formula relates this gateway to 'shareholder' profits.

* * *

The discussion was in three parts: the incentives of the long-term unemployed, the costs and impact of the targeted reflation, and the seriousness of the distortions caused by TIP to the operation of markets. Professor David Peel and a number from the floor queried the micro-economic basis of Jackman and Layard's analysis of the long-term unemployed; the fact that they do not affect wage increases in a 'Phillips curve' equation (relating wage increases to unemployment and other factors) needs to be explained in terms of their incentives, and any proposed schemes must then be shown to change their behaviour in a beneficial way.

For example, the long-term unemployed are for the most part unskilled and their supplementary benefits are therefore high relative to their potential earning power; their take-up even of Community Programme places has, perhaps as a result of this disparity, been disappointing. How would an extended programme overcome this problem without offering unrealistically high wages to induce these unemployed to take part? If such wages were offered as a special inducement to the long-term unemployed, would this not encourage people to remain unemployed for longer to qualify for these special inducements? Thus it was suggested the scheme could have a perverse effect on unemployment; and the costs would be much higher than the authors' estimates.

Both Peel and Brittan were concerned about the inflationary implications of the programme if realistically assessed in the light of these difficulties. The authors replied to these concerns by suggesting that the long-term unemployed were truly anxious for work at virtually any wage but were discouraged and discriminated against by employers solely because they had been on the dole for a long time; thus incentives would not be a problem, costs would be low,

---

[1]*An Incomes Policy to Help the Unemployed*, Employment Institute, 1986.

11

and so the reflation would pose no significant inflationary threat. This reply failed to convince those who asked why, if they were so keen to work at any wage, the long-term unemployed had not driven non-union wages down until jobs in this sector were made available to them. This important argument was not settled; clearly on the one side are those who believe there is some gap in the labour market through which the long-term unemployed have fallen, somehow unable to persuade any employer to take them at any price, and on the other side are those who suspect the market mechanism is there but is not being taken advantage of by the long-term unemployed because it does not pay them to do so.

Brittan raised concerns about TIP, widely shared on the floor; his own view was that wage/price restraint could at best be useful as a short-term emergency measure. Administrative feasibility in the narrow sense, as TIP is currently defined, might not be a problem, although the accounting wrangles in assessing gateway-eligible profits should not be under-estimated. But there would be numerous inequities between firms in the proposed PAYE formula. To take only one example, a firm expanding by taking on more executives could exceed the norm merely because it had an increasing proportion of relatively high-paid employees. This could generate as much protest as the supposed inflexibility of traditional incomes policy, bearing in mind the severity of the tax; presumably this would lead to more complex rules increasing administrative costs.

TIP would be little different in this respect from the traditional policies and could be expected to break down eventually under the same sort of stress. Turning to the impact of TIP, Peel took the authors to task for presenting TIP as a counter-inflation measure, which it clearly could not be. They agreed that TIP was not intended to be a substitute for control of the money supply; rather, its aim was indeed to reduce wage pressure *within* a framework of monetary restraint. Some participants then wondered whether TIP would not seriously impede expanding firms which needed to attract labour in short supply; the TIP penalty would particularly affect fast-growing service firms (such as information technology and financial services) which used skilled labour intensively and on which major hopes of employment creation are now centred. Growth in employment and output in these sectors would be reduced.

Another major concern was that efficiency would be penalised because wage increases could not be used as a reward for growth in productivity; the gateway permits profit-related pay but how widespread could such pay be among manual workers for whose efforts the link to profits is remote and who have generally rejected the instability in income implied by profit-related pay?

The authors recognised that all these points raised legitimate concerns. But they felt that quantitatively the disadvantages would not be too serious, and that the benefits of TIP in promoting employment by lowering wage pressures in labour markets where there was excess supply (especially for unskilled workers) would be seen to outweigh these disadvantages and create popular acceptance of TIP as a permanent fixture. This discussion leaves TIP to be judged on an empirical assessment of its balance of advantages, against those of alternatives.

4. Curing Unemployment through Labour-Market Competition

The last session turned to just such alternatives. Michael Beenstock and I argued that the agreed facts of the labour market—a high 'natural' rate of unemployment, including a lot of unskilled long-term unemployed, with little downward pressure on unskilled real wages—were consistent with a market analysis; benefits, taxes and earnings in the black economy depress incentives for the long-term unemployed to take regular jobs in the non-union sector, and union power keeps them out of the union sector where wages are kept well above the competitive norm. In one major economy, the USA, where these factors were weak or absent, real wages had barely risen and unemployment had stayed low—an instructive contrast to the UK. We also quote a number of formal studies of European economies supporting our analysis.

The policy emphasis in the paper is on the union aspect, where there has been progress on restrictive practices but, as recent studies attest, little impact has so far been made on union wage mark-ups. With about 80 per cent of workers covered by union agreements and 45 per cent of employees actually unionised, the elimination of union mark-ups by competition in the labour market would create many additional jobs by lowering union wages under the pressure of entry by workers currently excluded from the union sector; the long-term unemployed should be brought back into employment by this pressure because those entering the union sector would be leaving the non-union sector where wages would consequently rise, attracting into it those currently unemployed who have not hitherto found it attractive.

To this end, we propose a further tranche of union law reforms; we suggest that union immunities, already cut back, be withdrawn totally so that unions would once again be entirely within the domain of the common law. As a reserve measure, the labour market should come under the surveillance of the Monopolies and Mergers Commission (MMC); although theoretically empowered to do so, the MMC has never yet investigated labour practices. We argue finally that this 'competitive solution' has all the benefits claimed for TIP, without any of the distortions TIP would introduce.

* * *

Mr Jon Shields, with support from Professor Marcus Miller, suggested that unions had some beneficial effects; for example, in forcing inefficient managements to raise productivity, in opposing the monopoly power of employers in the labour market, and in enforcing the implicit contracts of workers with skills of little value outside the firm for which they were developed. Shields argued that corporatism, as evidenced in Austria and Scandinavia, was successful in keeping down unemployment as well as in economic management generally; this required much bigger and stronger unions than in the UK.

From the floor, Mr Graham Mather and Brittan wondered what sort of contracts and strike behaviour would emerge after the authors' proposed reforms. Would collective contracts not necessarily be referred to the MMC? Would formal individual contracts with a right-to-strike clause be negotiated? Professor Peter Sloane suggested that, if redundancies had by law to be random, majorities of union members would not vote for rises in real wages from whose job effects they are now protected by first-in-first-out redundancy. Although the desirability of restricting union monopoly power was generally recognised, there was concern about the political practicality of what could be seen as a frontal assault on the union movement.

As authors we acknowledge that unions could bring certain benefits, such as workers' voice, friendly society insurance, and so on; these advantages could survive the withdrawal of unions' monopoly powers. We were not proposing *abolishing* unions, merely bringing them within the common law and the scope of the MMC. As for policing contracts or inefficient and monopolistic managements, this sort of activity was best left to other processes, such as the law courts, the MMC, competition in goods markets, or take-overs. Corporatism had been tried in the UK and found wanting; our scepticism was widely shared on the floor, where it was pointed out that unemployment was also high in corporatist Benelux countries (low unemployment by contrast in Sweden was mainly due to the tough withdrawal of benefits after a certain duration of unemployment). Political practicability was a slippery concept; the 'impracticable' of today is often the 'obvious necessity' of tomorrow, as witnessed by attitudes to monetary control. Legislating for certain industrial relations practices (such as redundancies) in isolation was also likely to provoke effective union opposition, if unions' powers were left otherwise untouched. We were frankly unable to predict what type of constraints would emerge after our proposed reforms; in other words, the 'market would decide', but whatever it was we were confident it would be closer to the competitive norm, would not add to market distortions, and would increase rather than restrict individuals' economic freedom. There seemed a general willingness to move towards such competitive answers but residual scepticism about the politics of such radical reforms.

* * *

The conference thus ranged widely over issues of relevance to the macro-economic problems of the UK at the present time. It was conducted with scholarly frankness and scrupulous fairness to all points of view. We hope it will be a useful guide to these important issues.

1. Fiscal Policy in Britain: Placing the Medium-term Financial Strategy in Context

DAVID K. H. BEGG
Birkbeck College, London

With Commentaries by

ALAN BUDD
London Business School

and

DAVID CURRIE
Queen Mary College, University of London

The Author

DAVID K. H. BEGG was born in 1950 and educated at Kelvinside Academy, Glasgow, and St John's College, Cambridge. He is Professor of Economics and Head of the Economics Department at Birkbeck College, University of London, and a Research Fellow of the Centre for Economic Policy Research. From 1977–86 he was Lloyd's Fellow in Economics at Worcester College, Oxford. During periods of leave he taught at Princeton University in 1979, was Research Director at the Centre for Economic Forecasting at the London Business School during 1981–83, and was Adviser on Economic Policy Research in the Economics Division of the Bank of England during 1986–87.

Professor Begg is Managing Editor of *Economic Policy* and a former Senior Tutor of the Oxford University Business Summer School, on whose Steering Committee he now sits. He is also a member of H.M. Treasury's Academic Panel, and of the Research Advisory Awards Committee of the Leverhulme Trust.

His publications include *The Rational Expectations Revolution in Macroeconomics* (Philip Allan, 1982), *Economics* (with Rudiger Dornbusch and Stanley Fischer, McGraw Hill, 1984, 2nd edn. 1987), and papers on unemployment, financial markets, and macro-economic policy in professional journals.

I should like to thank David Currie, Rudi Dornbusch, Gareth Evans, John Flemming and Bob Gordon for helpful discussions, and Chas. Johnson for research assistance. All remaining errors are, of course, my own.

D.K.H.B.

I. INTRODUCTION

In the 1980s the Medium-Term Financial Strategy (MTFS) has become the centrepiece of fiscal policy under the Thatcher Government. In this paper I wish to place the MTFS in context by examining the evolution of British fiscal policy since 1970. Table 1 presents some familiar indicators of fiscal policy over that period. It shows a striking long-run increase in transfer payments (especially unemployment benefit) and a corresponding long-run increase in the pressure on government to finance expenditure by borrowing. The Table does *not* provide immediate evidence of large and sustained rises in exhaustive spending on goods and services, nor of increases in interest on debt or in revenue from taxes, much as all three are emphasised in the public debate.

Before 1970 such statistics would have been central to any evaluation of fiscal policy in practice. Since 1970 it is not merely the economy that has continued to develop; economic analysis itself has become considerably more sophisticated. On the one hand, economists now attach a good deal of importance to explicit examination of the government's 'budget identity'—the annual flows of spending, revenue and borrowing giving rise to the evolution of its stock of debt over time. On the other hand, analysis of decisions in both the government and the private sector now emphasises that such decisions are not myopic but rather are based on a forward-looking assessment of the medium to long run, in which expectations play a key role. Indeed, a complete definition of fiscal policy today requires an implicit specification of current and future government plans for spending, taxing and borrowing, including contingent plans to deal with future surprises.

TABLE 1

SIMPLE INDICATORS OF FISCAL POLICY, 1970-84
(% *of GDP at market prices*)

	1970	1973	1979	1984
Government spending on:				
Goods and services	22.3	23.1	22.4	23.8
Transfer payments	12.0	12.5	14.9	17.7
Debt interest	4.1	3.6	4.4	4.9
Taxes and other revenues	41.2	36.6	38.4	42.6
PSBR	0.0	5.6	6.4	3.5

Sources: Annual Abstract of Statistics; Economic Trends, HMSO.

Just as the definition of fiscal policy has altered since 1970, so has its focus. Demand management is no longer automatically the centrepiece. Why and how this change came about is the brief I have set for myself.

My story is organised as follows. Section II considers how to measure fiscal stance, that is, the impact of fiscal policy on aggregate demand. Section III reviews briefly the history of demand management in the UK, and the rationale for such policies. Section IV examines whether tight fiscal policy became required either for sound finance and the need to avert a domestic debt crisis, or for sound money to hold inflation in check. Section V discusses whether tight fiscal policy became necessary for supply-side reasons, that is, to improve the workings of markets. Conclusions are offered in Section VI.

II. INDICATORS OF FISCAL STANCE

The traditional role of fiscal policy was as an instrument of demand management. The systematic use of policy to reduce the fluctuations of output around its natural or potential level is possible only if two conditions hold. First, policy must have an impact effect on demand. Secondly, changes in aggregate demand must not contain the seeds of their immediate undoing through near-instantaneous induced changes in the prices of goods, labour, credit and foreign exchange.

In principle, both conditions may fail to hold. Here let me simply state that, whilst I believe both caveats to contain important insights, I regard them as much too extreme to be practical descriptions of the real world. Policy can affect aggregate demand, not least because the textbook assumption of perfect capital markets is nowhere close to practical fulfilment; and deviations from potential output are not immediately eliminated because short-run sluggishness of wage and price adjustment is a reality, for which modern macroeconomics is gradually providing a plausible rationale in the behaviour of individuals and firms.

In short, demand management is not an empty box or pointless exercise. If this is true, an indicator of fiscal stance is required to measure and hence evaluate the operation of demand-management in the UK since 1970. First, I must issue a series of important health warnings.

First, *no* indicator of fiscal policy can be chosen independently of an appropriate macro-economic model. For example, the consequence of a particular fiscal stimulus will depend critically on the initial level of involuntary unemployment (if any), the speed with which prices adjust, and the extent of imperfections in the capital markets. Secondly, no fiscal indicator can be independent of other *policies* in force. It will depend, for example, on the extent of monetary accommodation and on the exchange-rate régime. Thirdly, as I emphasised in my introduction, a complete description of fiscal policy requires a statement of current perceptions about future fiscal variables which, *inter alia*, requires a specification of how information evolves and expectations are formed.

Even in the abstract world of pure theory, there are precious few examples of models worked out in this degree of detail. Moreover, a realistic empirical index of fiscal stance would require a convincing macro-econometric model into which one could plug the evolution of beliefs about current *and future* fiscal actions, given similar beliefs about other policies in force. All this, however worthy an objective, would be a formidable undertaking.

For a practical assessment of UK fiscal policy since 1970 we are driven back on a measure which is considerably less sophisticated and, correspondingly, which must be interpreted with greater care and subtlety. I adopt a simple index of fiscal stance based on some elementary but important adjustments to the public sector financial deficit (PSFD). However, since they start from the contemporaneous deficit, they ignore the impact of expected future fiscal variables, the mix of fiscal and other policies, and the differing impact on demand of different spending and tax mixes within a given total deficit.[1]

First, an index of the 'real' deficit—that is, one properly adjusted for inflation—must go beyond the mere computation of the deficit at constant prices. Government spending includes nominal interest paid on the debt, and this transfer payment affects disposable incomes in the private sector. Yet, crudely, it is some measure of

---

[1] For an attempt to calculate a demand-weighted measure of the fiscal deficit, in which the impact on demand of separate tax and spending components are separately computed, Biswas, Johns and Savage [1985].

real-interest income which is relevant, as many studies of the consumption function confirm (for example, Davidson *et al.* [1978], Hendry [1983], and Patterson [1986]).

To measure 'real interest', one could, at one extreme, compute the *ex post* real short rate of interest and include only this element in the debt service component of the fiscal deficit. At the other extreme, one could appeal to perfect capital markets and permanent income, and value debt service at the *ex ante* long real interest rate on the outstanding debt stock. I adopt a simple compromise which values real debt service half way between the value obtained by using *ex post* real short interest rates and *ex ante* real long rates.

The second adjustment follows from the fact that some components of revenue and spending react to the business cycle. For example, policy sets rates of tax and welfare benefit but the consequent flows of expenditure and revenue depend on the level of GDP. To assess fiscal policy we need to think about the policy variables selected, not the subsequent expenditure and revenue flows. The most straightforward way to accomplish this is to compute the 'cyclically-adjusted deficit', showing what the deficit would have been had output been at its 'normal' or 'potential' level.

It is important to be clear how accurately the cyclically-adjusted deficit allows us to make inferences about fiscal stance and demand management. Suppose in a slump tax *rates* are temporarily reduced. Computing tax revenues as if output had been at potential will indeed reveal that discretionary policy had been relaxed in the slump and that demand management had indeed been practised. Thus variations in the cyclically-adjusted deficit over the cycle allow inferences about the direction of discretionary policy.

Having discussed the relevance of cyclical adjustment, I now select an index for the UK. Clearly, such an index depends both on a view of the potential output and on the model used to infer what the deficit would have been if output had attained this level in any particular year. I simply borrow the estimates computed by Muller and Price [1984].

Figure 1 shows my adjusted measure of the real fiscal stance combining the inflation-adjustment to the fiscal surplus and the cyclical correction discussed above. For comparison, it also shows the uncorrected surplus; the discrepancy between the two is striking. Whereas the naïve surplus suggests that fiscal policy has been expansionary, especially in the mid-1970s, the adjusted measure

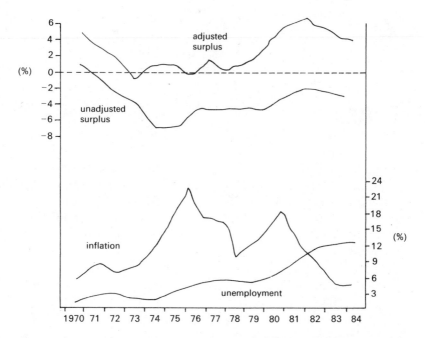

Figure 1: UK Public Sector Financial Surplus as Percentage of GDP, Unadjusted and Adjusted for Inflation and the Cycle, 1970-84

	Adjusted Surplus	Unadjusted Surplus	Inflation	Unemployment
1970	5.0	1.3	6.3	2.6
1971	3.3	− 0.5	9.4	3.5
1972	1.3	− 2.5	7.3	3.8
1973	− 1.0	− 3.8	9.1	2.7
1974	1.4	− 5.7	16.0	2.7
1975	1.1	− 7.2	24.2	4.1
1976	− 0.7	− 6.7	16.5	5.7
1977	1.5	− 4.2	15.5	6.2
1978	− 1.0	− 4.9	8.3	6.1
1979	0.9	− 4.4	13.4	5.6
1980	2.1	− 4.9	18.0	6.2
1981	5.3	− 3.6	11.9	9.5
1982	5.6	− 2.8	8.6	11.0
1983	3.7	− 3.6	4.6	12.1
1984	3.2	− 4.3	5.0	12.6

Sources: Muller and Price [1984]; Miller [1985]; *Economic Trends*, HMSO.

emphasises that fiscal policy was very tight in 1970, broadly neutral throughout the mid-1970s, and extremely tight again by the early 1980s. For reference, Figure 1 also shows the path of UK inflation and unemployment during the period.

III. FISCAL POLICY AND DEMAND MANAGEMENT, 1970-85

Although Table 2 provides the basic information from which a detailed assessment of demand management between 1970 and 1985 might be drawn, I prefer here to sketch the bare bones of policy during these years, to provide a skeleton which my subsequent discussion of the issues may be used to flesh out.

TABLE 2

BUDGET FORECASTS, OUTTURNS, AND FISCAL STANCE, 1970—84

Fiscal Year	Forecast GDP growth (%)	Actual outturn (%)	Forecasting error (%)	Cyclically adjusted real surplus (% of GDP)	Calendar Year
1970—71	3.5	2.0	−1.5	5.0	1970
1971—72	3.1	2.1	−1.0	3.3	1971
1972—73	5.9	8.9	3.0	1.3	1972
1973—74	4.5	−2.3	−6.8	−1.0	1973
1974—75	2.5	−0.7	−3.2	1.4	1974
1975—76	1.5	1.8	0.3	1.1	1975
1976—77	4.0	3.0	−1.0	−0.7	1976
1977—78	1.5	3.0	1.5	1.5	1977
1978—79	3.0	2.2	−0.8	−1.0	1978
1979—80	−1.0	−0.7	0.3	0.9	1979
1980—81	−1.5	−3.8	−2.3	2.1	1980
1981—82	1.0	0.7	−0.3	5.3	1981
1982—83	2.0	2.4	0.4	5.6	1982
1983—84	2.5	2.8	0.3	3.7	1983
1984—85	2.8	3.5	0.7	3.2	1984

Source: Financial Statement and Budget Report (various issues), HMSO, and Figure 1.

The Heath Government, 1970–74

Table 2 makes clear what a remarkably tight fiscal policy Edward Heath inherited from Labour in 1970. The Heath Government had been elected on a manifesto favouring market forces, the supply side, and a withdrawal from demand-management. Even so, fiscal policy was steadily relaxed in 1970-71, even before the famous policy U-turn in 1972, when the commitment to demand-management was formally re-adopted and both lame ducks and incomes policy were back in business.

The sustained fiscal expansion, evident from Table 2, coupled with an easy monetary policy, produced rapid growth in output. By 1973, domestic and international overheating had probably made accelerating inflation inevitable even without the forthcoming—and unforeseen—oil price shock. 1973 also saw the introduction of the only episode of wage indexation in recent UK history; this gave an ironic twist to the inflationary process.

The Wilson and Callaghan Governments, 1974-79

In 1974 most public attention was focussed not on the adverse implications for supply of the first oil shock but on how to neutralise its adverse effects on demand. In practice, this neutralisation was achieved largely by monetary accommodation. Table 2 shows that fiscal policy was only mildly contractionary in 1974-75, even given the legacy of the Heath boom and oil-induced inflation. Demand-management was still at the centre of the stage.

By 1976, the thrust of policy had begun to change in two respects. First, fiscal policy was no longer seen as the major *instrument* of demand-management; rather, following Kaldor [1971] policy aimed to secure an export-led expansion by trying to engineer a depreciation of the real exchange rate. Secondly, when this precipitated a sterling crisis, the government was prepared to subordinate reflation to the monetary and fiscal austerity required under the Declaration of Intent to the IMF in December 1976 as a condition for a massive IMF loan. Table 2 shows the sharp fiscal contraction of 1977. Thereafter, with unemployment mounting, fiscal policy was relaxed only slightly, and the uneasy truce with the unions continued until the 'Winter of Discontent' in 1978-79.

Thus, over the years 1974 to 1979 fiscal policy was broadly

25

neutral. The period did *not* show that demand management had ceased to work, as is sometimes asserted; rather, considerations of sound finance, credibility, and supply-side incentives had begun to emerge as issues of at least equal importance.

The Thatcher Government, 1979 onwards

With the relentless rise in unemployment, (correctly) attributed primarily to a deteriorating supply position, and the re-emergence of inflation after the winter of discontent, it is unsurprising that the Thatcher Government concluded that fiscal policy had more important objectives than demand-management.

The new government believed in supply-side economics, in the desirability of a credible anti-inflation strategy, and in the likelihood that output would usually be close to potential. So what was the new role for fiscal policy? First, to re-inforce the credibility of the MTFS and monetary control. Second, to stimulate the supply side through three channels: pre-emption of fewer resources for the state sector, lower tax rates, and lower borrowing which, it was hoped, would reduce interest rates.

In practice, this approach meant that fiscal policy started tight and had to become tighter. Table 2 shows the fiscal contraction of 1979. Coupled with the rapid sterling appreciation of 1979-81, this contraction generated an unexpectedly severe recession in 1980-81 and a PSBR overshoot. When in 1982 the government response was to *tighten* fiscal policy to restore the PSBR target, credibility was undoubtedly established and demand-management was not simply dead but buried.

The later Thatcher years have seen a gradual unwinding of this position of extreme stringency, both fiscally and in monetary policy. But it remains true, temporary electioneering aside, that demand-management is not an important consideration on the fiscal policy agenda.

The preceding remarks suggest that demand management has been displaced by concerns about inflation on the one hand and the supply side on the other. In the next two sections I examine these explanations in more detail.

IV. SOUND FINANCE AND A SOUND CURRENCY: DEBT, DEFICITS, MONEY AND INFLATION

Large deficits lead people to fear that the government will resort to finance through money creation, either immediately or in the future as the cumulation of debt interest exacerbates the deficit. Even worse, the government might have to default on its debt obligations. Do such fears provide a rationale for tight fiscal policy?

The Simple Arithmetic of the Public Accounts

The outstanding stock of public sector liabilities comprises the monetary base (MO, i.e. currency in the hands of banks and the private sector, plus banks' deposits with the Bank of England), bills, and bonds. In such a discussion, bonds should be assessed at market value, not at issue price: much of the subsequent analysis of unsound finance hinges on the possibility of using unanticipated inflation to inflict capital losses on private bondholders, for which it is necessary to assess government debt at market value.

Most discussion of the public debt focusses on the ratio of debt to GDP, which we might expect to be constant in a steady state. Binding debt to GDP captures the idea that, over time, the economy's capacity to service the debt at given tax rates will grow. Hence it is a crude attempt to make allowance for all the future variables which should be included in the analysis of public finances but are omitted.

Adopting the strong but useful assumption that the expected annual yields on bills and bonds are equal (implying that for bonds the coupon payment per pound invested plus the expected capital gain must equal the yield on bills), annual changes in the ratio of debt to GDP may be decomposed into four elements, each expressed as a fraction of nominal GDP. They are:

the primary deficit (spending minus taxes),
the adjusted cost of debt service (calculated from the excess of the short real interest rate over the rate of growth of real GDP),
the revenue raised from the creation of monetary base (the product of the growth of nominal GDP and the stock of high-powered money), and
the burden of *unanticipated* capital gains on outstanding bonds.

TABLE 3

NET PUBLIC DEBT AS A PERCENTAGE OF GDP, 1970—84
(*Selected years, and annual decompositions*)

	Net Debt/GDP (%)
1969	68.2
1973	48.9
1979	41.5
1984	41.0

contribution of, as per cent of GDP

	Δs	Primary deficit	Real money creation	Debt interest	Unanticipated capital gains
1970	−2.0	−3.5	−0.7	−1.2	3.6
1971	−7.9	−0.4	−0.8	−3.1	−3.9
1972	−2.9	0.1	−0.7	−2.0	−0.7
1973	−6.5	2.3	−0.9	−3.0	−3.6
1974	−6.3	3.5	−0.8	−0.2	−7.5
1975	−1.3	5.7	−1.3	−4.0	−0.4
1976	2.5	4.9	−0.9	−1.7	0.4
1977	1.8	2.3	−0.7	−2.2	2.0
1978	−3.7	0.4	−0.7	−1.5	−1.9
1979	−0.4	2.4	−0.7	−0.3	−0.8
1980	−3.2	2.0	−0.7	0.6	−5.2
1981	0.4	2.7	−0.4	1.0	−3.0
1982	0.7	−2.2	−0.4	1.5	1.1
1983	1.2	−0.2	−0.3	0.6	1.3
1984	0.4	0.0	−0.3	1.0	0.2
Annual Averages					
1970-73	−4.8	−0.4	−0.8	−2.4	−1.2
1974-79	−1.2	3.2	−0.8	−1.6	−1.4
1980-84	−0.1	0.5	−0.4	0.9	−1.1

Sources: Bank of England; Miller [1985].

Table 3 shows how the arithmetic of the public finances works out for the UK since 1970. It refers to UK public sector debt, net of certain fairly liquid public sector assets. The top part of the Table documents the dramatic reduction in the debt/GDP ratio since 1970, which merely continued a trend experienced during the post-war years, so that by the mid-1980s the UK had a lower debt/GDP ratio than many other OECD countries. In this simple sense it would be mistaken to believe that the UK had faced a crisis of the public finances which *required* the adoption of tight fiscal policy.

The lower part of Table 3 gives an annual decomposition of the elements which contributed to this trend, and displays annual averages for the approximate periods of office of the three governments since 1970. Several features deserve comment. First, the fastest reduction in the ratio of debt to GDP occurred during the Heath years; paradoxically, it has been slowest in the Thatcher years. Second, the differing contributions of the primary deficit (i.e. before debt interest) are not the main source of this conclusion. Third, revenue from money creation is typically small, being erected on a pinhead since the monetary base is tiny relative to GDP. Fourth, all three governments benefited from the unanticipated capital losses they inflicted on bondholders when nominal interest rates exceeded previous expectations. Finally, whereas the governments of the 1970s enjoyed real interest rates below the rate of real output growth, so that the debt burden was falling relative to GDP, in the 1980s high real interest rates have proved a significant burden on the public finances.

This last observation is of some importance. The existing debt is a burden on the public finances only when the real interest rate exceeds the rate of real output growth, as is surely a feature of the 1980s. But it is not obviously a feature of earlier decades, when real interest rates were often close to zero and sometimes negative and yet output growth was significant and sustained. In such circumstances, it would theoretically be possible to finance all public spending by borrowing, because the debt so created could always be expected to be absorbed by rising taxable capacity. When real interest rates rose, everyone had to start thinking about the medium-term programme by which the government would meet the real burden of its debt obligations. In these circumstances, a credible anti-inflation strategy requires that the government provides assurances today that it does not intend to resort to printing money tomorrow.

Although this analysis conveys important insights, it cannot purport to be a complete theory of why fiscal policy changed direction in Britain. As discussed above, concern about the PSBR and its possible implications for inflation dates back at least to the

29

mid-1970s when real interest rates were still significantly negative. Fear of inflation must play a more central role in the story. Before addressing that question directly, I wish to stress that neither the PSBR nor the ratio of debt to GDP provides an accurate indication of the soundness of the public finances.

Sound Finance and the Solvency of the Public Sector

While the debt of the public sector conveys some information about its liabilities, any assessment of its solvency must rest on a comparison of its liabilities and its assets. Such a criterion would, *inter alia*, eliminate the nonsense whereby asset sales (privatisation) appear to improve the public finances simply by reducing the PSBR and recorded debt outstanding. Privatisation may benefit the public finances, but any such benefit derives not from the transfer of ownership *per se*—selling an asset for the right price leaves wealth unaffected—but rather because associated changes in managerial efficiency or less stringent regulation of operating activities raises the market value of the asset.

Even tangible wealth is an inadequate measure of public sector net worth or solvency. The government also has the obligation to make future expenditure and the power to levy future taxation. Essentially, solvency requires that the initial stock of tangible wealth be at least as large as the present value of future operating deficits, suitably measured. Buiter [1985] gives a clear and comprehensive treatment of this issue.

Suppose one had a comprehensive annual measure of public sector net worth. The annual consumption stream it could sustain indefinitely would be given by this net worth multiplied by the long-run real interest rate. Thus a fiscal plan to consume more than this is implicitly a plan to leave subsequent governments with a worse fiscal position (Miller and Babbs [1983], Buiter [1985]).

Data on comprehensive public sector net worth do not exist. Where spending or revenue items are fairly constant over time, this year's value may be representative of future values too. But some items are known to be temporary and it is important to convert them to their permanent income or long-run equivalent value. I have in mind specifically oil and gas revenues from the North Sea. I make two further adjustments in the estimates presented below, the first taking account of the distinction between consumption and investment by the public sector, the second recognising the need to value debt interest at real, not nominal, interest rates.

Since I have argued that asset sales leave public net worth essentially unaffected, it is necessary to begin from the public sector financial deficit (PSFD), not the PSBR. As in Table 2, this figure should be adjusted for inflation, and instead of actual interest payments one wants to multiply the market value of net debt by the real interest rate, although this time it is the *expected* long rate which is relevant. Since the PSFD already includes rent on publicly owned dwellings and land, and since these rents may be thought of as index-linked, some crude allowance is already implicit for the role of non-financial assets.

Two further adjustments are required. First, using estimates from Devereux and Morris [1983] and Odling-Smee and Riley [1985] of the expected present value of oil revenues (which I assume to be close to zero prior to the first oil shock in 1973), I replace actual revenues with their contemporaneous permanent income value. Second, I make some allowance for the distinction between public consumption and investment. Some public investment (such as road building) yields no direct returns, although indirectly it may increase output and so tax revenues. This I treat as consumption. Whilst other public investment yields returns, it may (as an act of policy) have earned less than the full market rate. I therefore deduct from the PSFD one-half of public-sector expenditure on investment in dwellings and one-half of public corporations' investment. This adjustment errs deliberately on the cautious side. Column 6 of Table 4 thus shows, year by year, how much the fiscal plans were unsustainable.

The last two columns of Table 4 compare the adjusted index of the underlying public-sector surplus and the actual surplus cited in popular discussion. Whereas a naïve interpretation might suggest that the public finances were steadily deteriorating, the true position is strikingly different. The penultimate column reveals that the fiscal position improved dramatically in the early 1970s, and thereafter was steadily maintained until 1984.

Only in the mid-1980s, when revenue from North Sea oil substantially but temporarily exceeded its permanent income value, did fiscal policy exacerbate the problem of solvency for succeeding governments. These calculations of public-sector solvency provide no justification from sound finance for the adoption of tight fiscal

TABLE 4

THE PERMANENT-INCOME REAL SURPLUS OF THE PUBLIC SECTOR, 1970–84

| | £ million, current prices | | | As % of GDP | | | |
| | Oil & Gas Taxes | Permanent Income Equivalent | Public Investment | PSFS adjustment $(3)+(2)-(1)$ | PSFS at long real rate | Permanent income PSFS $(4)+(5)$ | Actual PSFS |
	(1)	(2)	(3)	(4)	(5)	(6)	(7)
1970	5	50	1,622	3.2	3.6	6.8	1.3
1971	10	75	1,668	3.0	1.5	4.5	-0.5
1972	15	100	1,781	2.9	-0.5	2.4	-2.5
1973	15	150	2,345	3.3	-1.6	1.7	-3.8
1974	20	630	2,930	4.2	-2.6	1.6	-5.7
1975	25	822	3,476	4.0	-4.3	-0.3	-7.2
1976	81	1,050	3,860	3.8	-3.6	0.2	-6.7
1977	238	1,230	3,532	3.1	-1.1	2.0	-4.2
1978	565	990	3,442	1.8	-1.9	-0.1	-4.9
1979	2,311	1,209	3,756	1.4	-1.2	0.2	-4.4
1980	3,735	2,532	4,063	1.2	-1.3	-0.1	-4.9
1981	6,491	3,105	3,298	0	0.2	0.2	-3.6
1982	7,814	3,090	3,175	-0.5	0.7	0.2	-2.8
1983	8,782	3,120	4,200	-0.5	-0.1	-0.6	-3.6
1984	12,002	3,120	4,605	-1.4	-1.0	-2.4	-4.3

Notes: (i) Estimate of contemporaneously calculated permanent income from oil and gas revenues based on Devereux and Morris [1983] and Odling-Smee and Riley [1985].

(ii) Public investment defined as one-half of the joint value of state corporations' investment and public sector investment in dwellings.

(iii) Column 5 taken from Miller [1985] who values debt service costs at the *ex ante* long real interest rate applied to all interest-bearing debt.

(iv) Column 7 shows actual public sector financial surplus as a percentage of GDP.

policy and the sacrifice of demand management at the date this transition actually occurred in the UK.

If the reasons for the adoption of a progressively tighter fiscal policy cannot be found in considerations of sound finance and the fear of impending insolvency, can we appeal instead to the need for sound money?

Inflation as a source of revenue

Inflation directly contributes to the government coffers through the inflation tax on the monetary base. Moreover, unanticipated inflation, by raising nominal interest rates, inflicts unanticipated capital losses on holders of nominal bonds, thus reducing the market value of the government's outstanding liabilities.

It is important to stress that in practice the revenue which can be raised through the inflation tax is small. First, notes and coin are now less than 4 per cent of UK GDP, and this ratio is in trend decline as financial innovations proceed apace. Second, the inflation tax, being the product of inflation and real high-powered money (the demand for which falls as inflation rises), has a theoretical maximum for most plausible specifications of money demand; thereafter revenue falls as inflation rises. Buiter [1985], for example, estimates that revenue is maximised when annual inflation is 67 per cent in the UK. But the central point is that this revenue will always be small (Table 3).

Table 3 also shows the effects of unanticipated changes in bond prices, the vast bulk of which revenue accrued from inflation effects on nominal bonds. Since the UK twice experienced years of inflation of roughly 20 per cent, which presumably was unanticipated when some of the nominal debt was first issued, Table 3 begins to give an idea of the once-off amount of revenue which a government could raise through this route.

To refine this question, it is vital to know more about the composition of the debt. The shorter the debt maturity, the less will the current price deviate from the par redemption value. Moreover, holders of indexed debt cannot be exploited at all through this mechanism.

The maturity structure of the UK debt has steadily shortened since 1970. Taken together with the increased trend for long debt to be index-linked, this implies a dramatic reduction in the possibility

of raising significant revenue through a bout of unexpected inflation. In part, this reflects a deliberate, and well-designed, credible
anti-inflation strategy for debt management, by seeking to commit
the government to a position in which it stands less to gain by any
subsequent unexpected inflation.

In the past, therefore, UK government finances have benefited
from inflation. Thus, if motivated by some other consideration,
UK governments that wished to effect a significant reduction in
inflation had to tighten other components of fiscal policy somewhat. But, since the underlying solvency of the public sector was
much healthier than popularly supposed, and given the *relatively*
small amounts of revenue which in any case had been raised
through inflation, it seems difficult to argue that fiscal policy in the
UK has been motivated by the desire to sustain the public finances
during a period in which inflation was being brought under control.

The Medium-Term Financial Strategy and Inflation

In 1980 the Thatcher Government adopted the Medium-Term
Financial Strategy (MTFS); it deserves special consideration.

The MTFS announced a three-year projection, annually
updated, for the PSBR as a percentage of GDP, on the understanding that any major revision of the initial projections would constitute a policy U-turn which the Government was pledged to avoid.
It was a simple form of commitment. The first six PSBR projections

TABLE 5
MTFS PROJECTIONS OF PSBR/GDP RATIO (%)

	1980/81	1981/82	1982/83	1983/84	1984/85	1985/86	1986/87
Targets							
80/81 Budget	3.75	3.00	2.75	1.50			
81/82 Budget		4.25	3.25	2.00			
82/83 Budget			3.50	2.75	2.00		
83/84 Budget				2.75	2.50	2.00	
84/85 Budget					2.25	2.00	2.00
85/86 Budget						2.00	2.00
Outturn	5.00	3.40	2.75	3.20	3.10	2.00	

Source: Financial Statement and Budget Report (various issues).

are set out in Table 5. The MTFS can be viewed in at least three ways: as a statement of the solvency of the fiscal position, as a device for monetary control whereby to control inflation, or as a more direct mechanism for tackling inflation.

(i) The MTFS as a statement of solvency
For reasons I have emphasised above, the PSBR/GDP ratio need bear no relation to the underlying sustainability of current levels of real consumption by the public sector at existing tax rates, nor to the sustainability of any other plan, including one to reduce the size of the public sector by a specified amount or to reduce marginal tax rates to particular levels.

(ii) The MTFS as reinforcement of monetary control
Did the MTFS represent instead an important strengthening of monetary control and a means of influencing inflation through this mechanism? Certainly its architects appeared to believe so at the time. Burns and Budd [1979] emphasised the demand-side linkage. By adding public debt to private portfolios, the PSBR would induce a rise in the portfolio demand for money, leading either to undesirable rises in interest rates or inflation if nominal money was allowed to increase. Yet this contention is dubious: even Milton Friedman believes that increases in the demand for real money balances can safely be accommodated without fear of inflation. Hence, if a budget deficit would have increased money demand and threatened to bid up interest rates, the appropriate policy response would simply have been to print more money to take the heat off interest rates. This extra money would have been held, not spent, and therefore would have had no inflationary consequences.

Others have emphasised linkages through money supply. In my view it is implausible that there *must* be a close connection between the PSBR and the money supply even over a period of several years. The monetary base is tiny relative either to other components of the government budget or to broad measures of money which might affect private behaviour. Any relation between deficits and the monetary base, at least over the range in which the UK has historically operated, is largely an outcome of deliberate policy, not of economic necessity. Even if such a relation did exist, the further links from MO to broad money (which is almost exclusively private bank deposits), and from there to inflation, are tenuous in the short and medium run.

For these reasons, I do not consider that the fiscal component of the MTFS was either necessary or sufficient for the conduct of a tight monetary policy which, especially during the first few years, the Thatcher Government believed central to the fight against inflation. The credibility of the Government's determination to sustain and win that fight was, of course, of the utmost importance. To paraphrase Fforde [1983], the fiscal component of the MTFS may have been less important for its underlying logic than in the fact that it was believed.

(iii) The MTFS in the direct control of inflation

I now want to argue that the MTFS contained an effective component which responded directly to inflation, and in two ways. The MTFS set targets for the path of the ratio of the nominal PSBR to nominal GDP; from these targets the Government would not budge, come what may. Table 5 confirms that subsequent revisions have been minimal, albeit with the help of some devices such as asset sales. I emphasised above that the PSBR/GDP ratio fails to adjust the PSBR for the effect of inflation in raising nominal interest rates. Unexpected inflation, therefore, automatically tightens the real fiscal stance, putting downward pressure on demand, prices and wages. Since this effect is guaranteed, it is a fairly credible signal that inflation will not subsequently get out of control.

The MTFS also contains a contingent promise to tighten other parts of fiscal policy when real interest rates rise. Hence it offers some assurance that corrective fiscal action will be taken, the public finances will remain sound, and reluctant money creation will be avoided. It seems to me that it is these contingent features of the MTFS which have the strongest logical appeal as part of an anti-inflation strategy and may in practice have contributed to its success.

V. FISCAL POLICY AND THE SUPPLY SIDE

By OECD standards, the UK's long-run growth performance had been poor and the steady rise in unemployment stemming from supply-side problems also led to a determination to attack these problems. My concern is the extent to which supply-side considerations motivated the macro-economic fiscal stance and the abandonment of demand management in Britain. Specifically, to what extent must a government choose *between* demand management and supply-side incentives.

Two arguments suggest that some trade-off does exist. First, higher marginal tax rates make automatic stabilisers more powerful in the short run but may lead to disincentive effects in the longer run. Second, Buiter and Miller [1983] have characterised the process as a 'game' between the government and the private sector. The co-operative solution, implicitly embodied in the 1944 Employment White Paper, is for the government to promise to manage demand and to commit itself to full employment whilst the private sector agrees to strive for growth of productivity combined with moderation in wage settlements. The co-operative solution is fragile precisely because, with such government commitments, the private sector faces two temptations to renege: it can go slow on productivity ('the easy life') without fear of unemployment, and it can push for higher wages knowing that in the short run this will lead to temporary real-wage increases while the commitment to subsequent monetary accommodation will inflate away these increases before serious adverse consequences for employment have time to feed through. In the language of modern 'dynamic game' theory, the co-operative solution may be 'time inconsistent': since the government can foresee that the private sector will face future temptations to renege, the government should abandon the wishful thinking embodied in the co-operative solution and design policy on the assumption that the private sector will renege.

Against this background, how should we interpret the fiscal choices made by UK governments since 1970? I agree with Buiter and Miller's characterisation of the 1950s and early 1960s as a period in which the fragile co-operative solution was sustained. Governments pursued active demand management with considerable success; in return, wage claims were moderate, inflation was low, and productivity growth was not so poor as to lead the government to conclude that this part of the bargain was in default.

With both inflation and unemployment increasing in the late 1960s, the Heath Government took office in 1970 on a manifesto which viewed the private sector—particularly the unions—as having begun to renege on both parts of their bargain. In consequence, it made sense for the government to reconsider its commitment to demand-management and the propping up of lame-duck firms by specific subsidies. Market forces were to be allowed to operate in the hope of disciplining an otherwise reluctant private sector.

For this policy to succeed, it was imperative that the Government should stick to its guns, and be expected to do so. In the event, as matters failed to improve quickly, political pressure forced the famous U-turn of 1972 in which demand management was unilaterally re-adopted—without any very credible commitment by the private sector to revert to co-operative behaviour. This U-turn, whether justified or not, was to have a profound effect on the subsequent design of policy. Specifically, Mrs Thatcher, who was adopted as leader of the Conservative Party in 1975, drew the obvious inference that mere promises to be tough were insufficient: a government embarking on such a course must first find a way to tie its own hands.

The period of Labour government from 1974 to 1979 should be divided into the sub-periods before and after 1976. During the Wilson years, demand was actively managed, albeit taking account of both the excessive 1973 boom and the deflationary impact of the first oil shock. Policy was primarily accommodating and known to be so. Nor did extravagant public-sector pay awards do anything to dispel the feeling that the government was adopting a distinctly co-operative posture in the belief (hope?) that the private sector would play ball.

Against this background, one should not under-estimate the change of direction undertaken by the Callaghan Government in 1976. (Callaghan's speech to the 1976 Labour Party Conference took as its theme the assertion that the expansion of demand would lead only to inflation, not to real growth of output.) In my judgement, the change in policy was intended primarily to reduce the inflationary bias which a guarantee of monetary accommodation had previously entailed. Public pronouncements notwithstanding, it is not clear that the government had really abandoned the management of demand of the real economy, as the active attempts to manage the real exchange rate during 1976 and 1977 attest.

Viewed in this light, the crucial innovation of the Thatcher Government was not the determination to fight inflation. Monetary targets for 1979-80 were barely tighter than those previously envisaged under Labour and, in both raising VAT and honouring the Clegg awards for public-sector pay increases, the 1979 budget deliberately added to inflation in the short run. Rather, its immediate innovation was to tackle incentives, productivity, and the supply side in general, significantly downgrading demand-management in favour of market forces. The real threat of unemployment and bankruptcies was intended to, and has, gradually changed attitudes among workers and managers. Mindful of the Heath U-turn, it was recognised that it was imperative to make this tough commitment credible. Initially, this was accomplished by persistent emphasis that there would be no U-turn, a strategy in which the government volunteered to punish *itself* for any subsequent reneging by so raising the political cost of such a reversal that it would not subsequently be able to undertake it. By 1980, this position was reinforced by the formal apparatus of the MTFS. When in 1981 the government responded to an unexpectedly severe recession (and consequent PSBR overshoot) by a severe fiscal contraction, its credibility had largely been established.

Necessarily, supply-side benefits will probably be slow to come through. What can undoubtedly be said without fear of contradiction is that the Thatcher Government has adopted a longer time-horizon, or lower discount rate on policy success, than previous governments. This should be regarded *per se* as a beneficial change in policy design.

VI. CONCLUSIONS

The two decades before 1970 saw a consensus in macro-economic policy in which the pursuit of full employment and demand management was paramount, and fiscal policy played a central role. During the 1970s, the combination of high inflation, steadily rising unemployment, and, after 1973, sluggish growth of output gradually convinced policy-makers that demand management should be subordinated to other objectives of fiscal policy. This reassessment did not begin with Margaret Thatcher but its implications were most clearly and determinedly pursued during her government, when the fiscal stance was very tight even though output was well below potential. Demand-management had been almost completely abandoned.

Considerations of sound finance do not provide a very plausible rationale for this change in emphasis in fiscal policy. The popular debate deals in indicators which bear little relation to a true assessment of the sustainability of fiscal policy. The public finances have been considerably more healthy than is commonly supposed. Nor has a tight fiscal policy been essential for pursuit of a monetary policy which would bring inflation under control. Even so, the fiscal component of the MTFS may have reinforced beliefs that the government intended to win the fight against inflation. And it did contain an implicit commitment to tighten fiscal policy if inflation should unexpectedly rise.

To an important extent the adoption or maintenance of tight fiscal policy during a major recession was specifically designed to signal the end of the commitment to demand-management in the hope that this stance would alter private behaviour and gradually improve supply-side performance.

During the 1980s, the performance of the UK in reducing inflation has improved substantially. Yet to date neither this nor the attack on supply-side problems has led to any significant improvement in the real economy. The failure to use fiscal policy to stimulate demand in the early 1980s undoubtedly led to a sacrifice of output. It remains to be seen whether the UK will recoup this output with interest.

REFERENCES AND RELATED READINGS

Allsopp, C. J. and D. G. Mayes [1985]: Chapters 12 and 13 in D. Morris (ed.), *The Economic System in the UK*, Oxford University Press, Oxford.

Artis, M. and D. Currie [1981]: in W. A. Eltis and P. J. N. Sinclair (eds.), *The Money Supply and the Exchange Rate*, Oxford University Press, Oxford.

Barro, R. J. [1974]: 'Are Government Bonds Net Wealth?', *Journal of Political Economy*.

Biswas, R., C. Johns, and D. Savage [1985]: 'The Measurement of Fiscal Stance', *National Institute Economic Review*.

Blanchard, J. [1985]: 'Debts, Deficits, and Finite Horizons', *Journal of Political Economy*.

Britton, A. J. C. [1986]: 'Can Fiscal Expansion Cut Unemployment?', *National Institute Economic Review*.

Brown, C. V. [1980]: *Taxation and the Incentive to Work*, Oxford University Press, Oxford.

Bruno, M. [1986]: 'Sharp Disinflation Strategy: Israel 1985', *Economic Policy*.

Buiter, W. H. [1980]: 'The Macroeconomics of Dr Pangloss', *Economic Journal*.

Buiter, W. H. [1985]: 'A Guide to Public Sector Debt and Deficits', *Economic Policy*.

Buiter, W. H. and M. Miller [1981]: in W. A. Eltis and P. J. N. Sinclair (eds.), *The Money Supply and the Exchange Rate*, Oxford University Press, Oxford.

Buiter, W. H. and M. Miller [1983]: 'The Macroeconomic Consequences of a Change in Regime: the UK under Mrs Thatcher', *Brookings Papers on Economic Activity*, The Brookings Institution, Washington DC.

Burns, T. and A. Budd [1979]: 'The Role of the PSBR in Controlling the Money Supply', London Business School.

Caves, R. E. *et al.* [1968]: *Britain's Economic Prospects*, The Brookings Institution, Washington DC.

Cohen, D. [1985]: 'How to Evaluate the Solvency of an Indebted Nation', *Economic Policy*.

Cohen, D. and J. Sachs [1984]: 'Growth and External Debt under Risk of Debt Repudiation', External Debt Division, World Bank, Washington DC.

Davidson, J. *et al.* [1978]: 'Econometric Modelling of the Aggregate Time Series Relationship between Consumers' Expenditure and Income in the UK', *Economic Journal*.

Devereux, M. and C. N. Morris [1983]: 'The Pattern of Revenue Receipts from North Sea Oil', *Fiscal Studies*.

Flemming, J. S. [1973]: 'The Consumption Function when Capital Markets are Imperfect: the Permanent Income Hypothesis Reconsidered', *Oxford Economic Papers*.

Fforde, J. [1983]: 'Setting Monetary Objectives', *Bank of England Quarterly Bulletin*.

Friedman, B. M. [1985]: 'The Effect of Large Government Deficits on Interest Rates and Equity Returns', *Oxford Review of Economic Policy.*

Hendry, D. F. [1983]: 'Econometric Modelling: The "Consumption Function" in Retrospect', *Scottish Journal of Political Economy.*

Hills, J. [1984]: 'Public Assets and Liabilities and the Presentation of Budgetary Policy', in M. Ashworth, J. Hills, and C. N. Morris (eds.), *Public Finances in Perspective*, Institute for Fiscal Studies.

Kaldor, N. [1971]: 'Conflicts in National Economic Objectives', *Economic Journal.*

King, M. A. [1985]: 'Tax Reform in the UK and in the US', *Economic Policy.*

King, M. A. and D. Fullerton [1984]: *The Taxation of Income From Capital: A Comparative Study of the United States, United Kingdom, Sweden, and West Germany*, University of Chicago Press, Chicago.

Kydland, F. E. and E. C. Prescott [1977]: 'Rules rather than Discretion: the Inconsistency of Optimal Plans', *Journal of Political Economy.*

Layard, P. R. G. *et al.* [1984]: *The Case for Unsustainable Growth*, Centre for European Policy Studies, Economic Paper No. 31.

Layard, P. R. G. and S. J. Nickell [1985]: 'The Causes of British Unemployment', *National Institute Economic Review.*

Miller, M. H. [1982]: 'Inflation-adjusting the Public Sector Financial Deficit', in J. A. Kay (ed.), *The 1982 Budget*, Blackwell, Oxford.

Miller, M. H. [1985]: 'Measuring the Stance of Fiscal Policy', *Oxford Review of Economic Policy.*

Miller, M. H. and S. Babbs [1983]: 'The True Cost of Debt Service and the Public Sector Financial Deficit', mimeo, Bank of England.

Muellbauer, J. and L. Mendis [1983]: 'Employment Functions and Productivity Change: Has there been a British Productivity Breakthrough?', Centre for Economic Policy Research, Discussion Paper.

Muller, P. and R. W. R. Price [1984]: 'Structural Budget Indicators and the Interpretation of Fiscal Policy Stance in OECD Economies', *OECD Economic Studies.*

Odling-Smee, J. and C. Riley [1985]: 'Approaches to the PSBR', *National Institute Economic Review.*

Patterson, K. D. [1986]: 'The Stability of Some Annual Consumption Functions', *Oxford Economic Papers.*

Pissarides, C. [1986]: 'Unemployment and Vacancies in the UK: Facts, Theory, and Policy', *Economic Policy.*

Sargent, T. J. [1981]: 'Stopping Moderate Inflations: the Methods of Poincaré and Thatcher', mimeo.

Sargent, T. J. and N. Wallace [1981]: 'Some Unpleasant Monetarist Arithmetic', Federal Reserve Bank of Minneapolis, *Quarterly Review.*

Sargent, J. R. and M. Fg. Scott [1986]: 'Investment Incentives and the Tax System in the UK', *Midland Bank Review* Spring.

Tobin, J. [1961]: 'Money Capital, and Other Stores of Value', *American Economic Review.*

Tobin, J. [1969]: 'A General Equilibrium Approach to Monetary Theory', *Journal of Money, Credit and Banking.*

Yarrow, G. [1986]: 'Privatisation in Theory and Practice', *Economic Policy.*

Commentary-1
ALAN BUDD
London Business School

I have found this an interesting paper, as I would have expected. I can also say, at the outset, that I have no quarrels with the theory. I shall limit my comments to two points. The first concerns the measurement of the fiscal stance and the second focusses on the role of fiscal policy in the MTFS.

1. Measuring the Fiscal Stance

David Begg makes a number of adjustments to the figures for the PSBR in order to obtain a more useful measure of the fiscal stance. Some of these adjustments are familiar enough. For example, it is sensible to try to measure changes in the 'structural deficit' by removing endogenous changes due to changes in GDP. As Begg correctly remarks, this does not necessarily tell us what degree of stabilisation has been attempted since various structures of taxes and state spending will have widely differing degrees of 'built-in' stabilisation. In this context it is also sensible to remove asset sales from the PSBR since it is difficult, if not impossible, to defend their definition as 'negative public spending'.

The adjustment which worries me is that for inflation. Its rationale is that part of state spending consists of interest payments on public-sector debt. If there is inflation, nominal rates of interest will include payments to allow for maintenance of the real value of loans to the government. The deficit should therefore be adjusted to allow for the effects of inflation. If the object of the exercise is to measure the degree of demand stimulation achieved by the government's activities (*ex post*), it is correct to make this adjustment; but I believe it is wrong to argue that the resulting figure measures the stance of fiscal policy.

Nominal and real values
An analogy with monetary policy may be helpful. In giving evidence to the House of Commons Treasury and Civil Service Committee, Mr Frank Cassell of the Treasury distinguished

between 'monetary policy' and 'monetary conditions'.[1] The distinction broadly corresponds to the difference between the nominal and real values of policy variables. If the government chooses to reduce inflation by cutting nominal monetary growth, the immediate effect, before inflation adjusts itself, will be for the growth of real money balances to slow down. As inflation falls, real monetary growth, for a given nominal monetary growth, will accelerate. This can be described as a change in monetary conditions but it would be wrong to describe it as a change in monetary policy.

Let us suppose that the government chooses to accompany its reduction in monetary growth with a reduction in the nominal value of the public-sector financial deficit, expressed as a share of GDP. If inflation does not adjust itself immediately, and if there is government debt which is not index-linked, the immediate fall in the inflation-adjusted deficit is larger than the long-run fall. The inflation-adjusted deficit (as a share of GDP) will therefore rise as inflation falls. However, it would be quite wrong, in my view, to interpret this as a change in the fiscal stance. Fiscal conditions have eased but fiscal policy is unchanged. In the present context, the reduction in inflation was an intended consequence of the original reduction of the deficit. It seems odd, therefore, to claim, as some commentators have done recently (though not Begg), that the recovery of output since 1981 is the result of a change in government policy (as measured by the inflation-adjusted deficit). There may have been a relaxation of fiscal policy but the inflation-adjusted deficit cannot be used to measure it.

This interpretation was questioned during discussion by Mr Henry Neuberger, who made the following point: Suppose there is an autonomous rise in inflation, which the government does not accommodate; such a rise will reduce the real value of the deficit (and of monetary growth). Can one then say that there has been no change in fiscal policy or should one accept that fiscal *policy* (as well as fiscal *conditions*) have been tightened?

As in all such matters, it is obviously wrong to be dogmatic about definitions. My own view is that, as far as possible, policy should be defined in nominal terms. Thus I would describe an unanticipated acceleration of inflation as a tightening of fiscal and monetary

---

[1] Fifth Report from the Treasury and Civil Service Committee, Session 1982–3: *The 1983 Budget*, HC286, HMSO, 1983, p. 14.

conditions rather than as a tightening of policy. But I would not expect the use of words to pre-empt the serious question of whether government should change its nominal policy in response to unanticipated changes in inflation. Thus a government that refused to accommodate inflation could not simply defend its actions by saying that it had not tightened its policy. It is consequences of actions that matter, not the labels that economists attach to them. (By the same token, a government could not defend a decision to accommodate inflation by arguing that, on its definition, policy was unchanged.)

2. Fiscal Policy and the Medium-Term Financial Strategy

Much of Begg's paper is concerned with asking why the Conservative Government incorporated a path for fiscal policy in the MTFS. Although I found this discussion interesting, I also found it rather puzzling. This confusion arose partly because I was not sure whether he was interested in *his* rationale for what was happening or in the Government's rationale. He considered a number of possibilities and rejected them.

He argues that it cannot have been because of fears of fiscal instability since, at the time the MTFS was introduced, real rates of interest were negative and the Government, in principle, had limitless borrowing powers. As a matter of theory I am sure he is right. He is also correct as a matter of history. Concerns about the size of the debt and risks of instability were not raised for several years. Also they were raised outside Whitehall, particularly by Tim Congdon.[2]

Begg next considers the possibility that the Government had to tighten fiscal policy because it faced (if its policies were successful) the loss of its inflation tax. Again, he rejects this argument—and he is right to do so. I find it hard to believe this was a serious concern for the Government, and Begg shows that it was relatively unimportant in quantitative terms.

He concludes that the adoption of a tight fiscal policy represented a change in the rules of the game. The Government declared, in effect, that it would no longer ensure full employment if employers and employees made mistakes in setting prices and

---

[2] T. Congdon, 'The Analytical Foundations of the Medium-Term Financial Strategy', *Fiscal Studies*, Vol. 5, No. 2, May 1984.

wages. By establishing nominal targets for the PSBR the Government provided a built-in stabiliser against any tendency for inflation to move ahead more rapidly than intended. While that may provide a coherent rationale for what happened, I do not believe it explains why the Government chose to announce a path for the PSBR at the same time that it presented its targets for the money supply. But there is no call for speculation about the Government's reasons since it has presented them many times, in Budget speeches, in successive editions of the *Financial Statement and Budget Report*, in the Mais Lecture, in Mansion House speeches, in evidence to the Treasury and Civil Service Committee, and so on and on.[3]

The first presentation of the MTFS, in the *Financial Statement and Budget Report* of 1980, provides a full account:

'It is not the intention to achieve this reduction in monetary growth by excessive reliance on interest rates. The government is therefore planning for a substantial reduction over the medium term in the Public Sector Borrowing Requirement (PSBR) as a percentage of Gross Domestic Product (GDP). The relationship between the PSBR and the growth of money supply is important but is not a simple one; it is affected by the economic cycle, the rate of inflation and the structure of the tax and public expenditure flows generating the borrowing requirement.

But although the relationship between the PSBR and £M3 is erratic from year to year, there is no doubt that public sector borrowing has made a major contribution to the excessive growth of the money supply in recent years. The consequence of the high level of public sector borrowing has been high nominal interest rates and greater financing problems for the private sector. Even in the context of rapid inflation, high nominal interest rates are a deterrent to investment. If interest rates are to be brought down to acceptable levels the PSBR must be substantially reduced as a proportion of GDP over the next few years'.[4]

What could be clearer than that? Begg refers to this argument briefly and dismisses it. As a matter of history I think he wrongly describes the views presented by Terry Burns and me (whom he describes as the architects of the strategy). There are two ways of describing the link between the PSBR and the money supply: the first concerns the supply of money, and the second the demand for

---

[3] For example, Nigel Lawson, 'The British Experiment', The Fifth Mais Lecture, 18 June 1984.
[4] *Financial Statement and Budget Report 1980–81*, HC500, HMSO, 1980.

money. The supply-of-money approach relies on the monetary identities. For purposes of argument we can rely on the simplified version of the identity as follows:

change in money supply (M3) = PSBR *plus* advances *minus* sales of government debt to non-monetary sector

It follows from this identity that the attempt to hold down the growth of the money supply while maintaining a large PSBR will succeed only if interest rates are high enough to discourage bank advances and to encourage sales of government debt. If the government is unwilling to allow interest rates to rise sufficiently, it will be unable to control the growth of the money supply. Burns and I were relying on that argument.

The demand-side approach
I associate the demand-side approach with the Treasury and the Bank of England. This approach starts from the rise in government assets held by the private sector as a result of high public-sector borrowing requirements. The rise in public-sector debt will in turn lead to a rise in the demand for money by the private sector in order to preserve portfolio balance. Either this demand will result in an unacceptable rise in the growth of the money supply, or it will result in unacceptably high interest rates.

The two approaches are not inconsistent, but the second approach does not rely on the monetary identities. In each case the fundamental problem is one of portfolio equilibrium and the risk of higher interest rates if the government tries to drive a wedge between the size of the PSBR and the growth of the money supply. (In the long term or 'steady state', government debt and the money supply must be growing at the same rate. On the path to the new steady state, the ratio of government debt to money balances will rise continuously.)

Since the Government wanted to reduce interest rates, it believed it had to avoid the possible problem caused by changes in portfolio balances. Its monetary policy had therefore to be accompanied by a consistent fiscal policy. Begg dismisses both approaches. Against the supply-side approach he argues that the monetary identity is in practice a weak constraint, particularly in the short term. Against the demand-side approach he quotes Milton Friedman. Yet Friedman himself argues that the excess demand for money may have to be squeezed out by a rise in interest rates—a consequence the Government wants to avoid.

* * *

In discussion, two points were raised. The first was that, despite the reductions in the PSBR/GDP ratio, real interest rates had risen since the MTFS was introduced. Any economist will know how to reject that argument.[6] The second was that since the UK was a small open economy, it could borrow all it wanted at world interest rates. That is an empirical question but it would seem reasonable to suppose that loans to the UK were not a perfect substitute for loans to all other countries, and that the UK would face an upward-sloping supply curve for loans, implying rising UK real interest rates the more it borrowed abroad.

There is a further point that can be made about the role of fiscal policy in the UK. Even before 1980 (since when events have made it so evident), few believed there was a simple short-term relationship between the money supply (on a broad definition such as £M3) and nominal GDP. Even if there were, the Government still had to consider the impulse it was providing to nominal GDP by its fiscal policy. If fiscal policy implied a growth of nominal GDP which was inconsistent with the Government's monetary targets, the resulting pressure on financial markets would have implications for interest rates and hence for the allocation of resources which might well conflict with other aspects of government policy.

I conclude that the role of fiscal policy in the MTFS has been neither mysterious nor irrational. That does not mean that it has been an easy matter to choose the correct nominal targets, but the Government's approach to counter-inflationary policy has meant that it could not rely on monetary policy alone.

---

[6] I.e., other things were *not* equal.—ED.

Commentary-2
DAVID CURRIE
Queen Mary College, University of London,
and Centre for Economic Policy Research

It is a pleasure to have the opportunity of discussing Professor Begg's paper. I have a stereotyped image of IEA papers as being thought-provoking but somewhat hare-brained, and in that respect Begg's paper surprises with its combination of intelligence, insight and level-headedness. I agree with much of Begg's analysis, and so in what follows I shall focus mainly on points of difference.

Begg's empirical analysis follows Buiter [1985] in focussing very much on the inflation-adjusted and cyclically-adjusted fiscal deficit, and on the permanent income deficit, corresponding to changes in public sector net worth. I agree that these measures are important, but I am sceptical about exclusive reliance upon them. If one is concerned with the effects of fiscal policy on aggregate demand (played down in Begg's analysis), the relevance of the adjustment for inflation depends largely on the incidence of the inflation tax: if it falls mainly on financial institutions, short-run movements in this adjustment may have rather minor effects on expenditures.

Moreover, the different components of public expenditure and taxation making up the fiscal deficit have quite different implications for demand, and it is important to allow for this difference by a suitably weighted measure. The permanent income deficit is not useful for considering questions of impact on aggregate demand, for it ignores potential failures of the capital market (through asymmetric information, moral hazard and adverse selection) that drive a wedge between government and private borrowing rates. For these reasons, I would have preferred a more multi-dimensional approach to the appraisal of fiscal policy.

Treatment of investment in public infrastructure

I am sympathetic to Begg's use of the comprehensive balance-sheet approach to the public sector, which brings into account real sector assets alongside financial liberties. But I have some reservations about treating as consumption the component of public investment which yields no pecuniary return, as Begg does. To take the usual example, a failure to replace deteriorating sewers may unleash a very expensive train of developments in the future. It is not appropriate to regard a decision *not* to renew public infrastructure as enhancing public-sector net worth, representing prudential financial management. Yet that is the effect of Begg's calculations. In many circumstances, the decision to invest in infrastructure would lead to a lower permanent income deficit, properly measured. Moreover, there is surely a strong argument, on grounds of intergenerational equity, that, if a government were replacing sewers that are expected to last another 100 years, such investment should be financed by long-term government borrowing, to be serviced out of taxes over the lifetime of the new sewers.

Similar arguments apply to other public-sector infrastructural investment. For these reasons, the decline in public-sector infrastructural investment under Mrs Thatcher's Governments cannot be regarded as financially prudent. Conversely, there are sound arguments for stepping up such investment at the present, and financing it by long-term public borrowing.

Supporting roles for fiscal policy

Turning now to the main thrust of Begg's paper, he argues that fiscal policy had two main roles under the Medium-Term Financial Strategy (MTFS): first, to enhance the credibility of the MTFS by abandoning demand management; second, to improve the supply side of the system.

To begin with the supply side, Begg identifies three supporting roles for fiscal policy:

(i)   pre-empting fewer resources for the public sector;
(ii) reducing taxation; and
(iii) lowering interest rates by reducing government borrowing.

In these roles, the conduct of fiscal policy has flopped. As Begg shows in his Table 1, public expenditure on goods and services has risen, both absolutely and as a proportion of GDP. This is also true of the overall tax burden, despite recent Budgets. And, of course, real interest rates are now unprecedentedly high. In these aspects, the MTFS has not delivered.

Moving on to questions of demand-management, Begg argues

that supply-side considerations motivated the abandonment of demand-management. The first reason he gives is that high marginal tax rates make automatic fiscal stabilisers more powerful, but have disincentive effects (although theory suggests that even the sign of these effects is ambiguous, and empirical evidence for their presence is not cited). It is interesting to note that the same point does not apply to the discretionary use of tax changes to stabilise demand, because discretionary increases in taxes in response to *aggregate* movements of income are in no way inconsistent with low marginal rates of tax and an absence of disincentive effects on the individual. Building the tax responsiveness to demand into the tax system requires the responsiveness to be built into the individual's tax schedule; while a discretionary response allows the link to be established only in the aggregate, with negligible consequences for individual incentives. This illustrates a more general point, that rigidity and automaticity in policy design may be unduly restrictive.

MTFS 'threat strategy'—a failure?

The second reason Begg gives for a trade-off between demand-management and supply-side considerations is related to the role of the MTFS as a 'threat strategy' in a game between the Government and the private sector. By abandoning demand-management, the Government signalled a commitment to deal with inflation by market forces, if necessary allowing unemployment and bankruptcies to contain wage and price inflation.

I suspect that there is a lot of truth in this interpretation of the MTFS. The question, which Begg does not answer, is whether it has been deployed successfully in this role. In answering it, the economist ought to remember that, as all parents know in their relationships with their children, the best threats are those that do not have to be carried out. Yet unemployment has risen massively during the period of the MTFS, while the growth of real earnings has remained high. It is hard to resist the conclusion that the Government's bluff was called and that it failed to deliver. There are, moreover, good reasons that this failure was to be expected. The threats analysed by Begg are of an aggregate kind that relate aggregate policy to aggregate performance. As such, individuals do not perceive these threats as impinging on them personally. (They might impinge on large collective groupings, such as trade unions, but the influence of such groupings has been weakened by other parts of government policy.) Because of this, the threat strategy had no bite.

There was a time when it appeared that the Government's response to this would be to administer more of the same (rather like some players in experimental prisoners' dilemma games who doggedly press the 'non-co-operate' button, come what may). But in the last two years the Government has been wriggling out of the straitjacket imposed by the MTFS, paying more attention to the exchange rate and undertaking a fiscal expansion under cover of asset sales. The question, then, is what we should learn from this episode. There is a danger that this period will be used to discredit a 'rule-driven' conduct of macro-economic policy. I am sure that is the wrong conclusion. Instead, we should be considering more flexibility in the design of our rules for macro-economic policy. Such flexibility may well enhance, not reduce, credibility and improve macro-economic performance (Artis and Currie [1981]). That is the issue raised by the failures of the MTFS.

REFERENCES

Artis, M. J. and Currie, D. A. [1981]: 'Monetary Targets and the Exchange Rate: A Case for Conditional Targets', *Oxford Economic Papers,* Vol. 33, Supplement, pp. 176–200.

Buiter [1985]: 'A Guide to Public Sector Debt and Deficits', *Economic Policy.*

2. Monetary Indicators and Operating Targets
Some Recent Issues in the UK

R. A. BATCHELOR
Centre for Banking and International Finance,
The City University Business School, London

With Commentaries by

C. A. E. GOODHART
London School of Economics and Political Science

and

HAROLD ROSE
Economic Adviser, Barclays Bank

The Author

ROY BATCHELOR is Reader in Economics in the Centre for Banking and International Finance at The City University Business School, London, and Director of the City Institute for Financial and Economic Research. After obtaining a First Class Honours degree in Economics and Statistics from Glasgow University, Mr Batchelor worked as an economist in government, and at the National Institute of Economic and Social Research. He is the author of books on industrialisation and trade, exchange rate policy, and protectionism, and of many articles on trade and exchange rate policy, monetary control, and inflation expectations.

I. INTRODUCTION AND SUMMARY

Since the promulgation of the Medium-Term Financial Strategy (MTFS) in the 1980 Budget, macro-economic policy in the United Kingdom has revolved around the Thatcher Government's attempts to reduce inflation by means of a progressive, pre-announced reduction in the rate of growth of the money supply. This paper surveys the main issues of strategy and, more especially, monetary control tactics which have arisen during the period of implementation of this 'monetarist' policy.

The MTFS makes sense only within a particular view of how the economy works, and the monetary policy component of the MTFS is only part of a broader package of measures indicated by the monetarist model—measures which include a compatible fiscal policy and supportive micro-economic measures aimed at improving efficiency in the real economy. I first set out the essential elements of the monetarist model. This is deliberately done in a highly stylised way, in order to bring a number of issues surrounding the conduct of monetary policy into sharp focus.

I shall then go on to criticise two aspects of the Government's handling of monetary policy. The first is related to their reaction to the breakdown of Sterling M3 (£M3) as an indicator of inflationary trends. This proved a difficult problem, since the breakdown, while partly the result of bad policy, was largely because of unprecedented changes in the structure of the banking system. But the response of the authorities in publishing a profusion of alternative indicators in successive budgets betrays a misunderstanding of the key role of this target as a focus for inflationary expectations.

The other criticism concerns the terms of the debate over operating procedures for monetary control. Although the monetarist model which underpins the MTFS emphasises the importance of money growth for inflation, the authorities have persisted in using a framework of monetary analysis which emphasises credit rather than money. Similarly, while the criteria for choosing between interest rates, the monetary base, and the exchange rate as an operating target are equally clearly indicated by the theory—it is all a matter of whether interest rate, price, or exchange rate uncertainty is most damaging—the debates over techniques of monetary control and Britain's membership of the European Monetary System (EMS) have not been conducted in these terms. Rather, they have focussed on short-term considerations, such as the benefits from pegging sterling below its supposed equilibrium value.

Again, in order to highlight these issues, I have adopted a deliberately critical viewpoint. However, I do not want to leave a negative impression regarding the overall conduct of monetary policy. The Thatcher Government has clearly done something right, in bringing inflation to low single figures, and in breaking the high-inflation mentality of the 1970s. My concern is simply that, by better monetary management, these gains could perhaps have been bought at less cost in reduced output and increased uncertainty.

II. THE MONETARIST MODEL

The basic assumption of the monetarist model is that the total activity in the economy, and aggregate prices, are determined in the same way as quantities and prices in individual markets, by the interaction of demand and supply. It is further assumed that aggregate demand for and supply of the real output of the economy react to monetary conditions in fairly specific ways.

The growth rate of demand usually proceeds at some trend rate. It may be driven above or below this trend, however, if the growth in the stock of real money balances in the economy (the difference between money growth and the inflation rate) exceeds or falls short of the growth in demand by the public to hold the real money stock. Aggregate demand may also be subject to random shocks, positive or negative. An unexpected exchange rate appreciation is an example of such a shock.

Growth of demand, spending and trend ('permanent') income

The trend growth in demand can be thought of as resulting from the tendency of individuals and firms to gear spending, on consumption and investment, to an estimate of trend income ('permanent' income, in Milton Friedman's phrase) or output growth rather than the more volatile current income growth. The impact of money growth on real demand can be regarded either as arising from individuals attempting to reduce excess real money balances by spending the money directly on goods; or by their spending the excess money on bonds, thus lowering interest rates and indirectly raising the demand for (investment) goods.

The growth of supply also usually proceeds at some trend natural rate. Supply may be driven above or below this trend, however, if the actual rate of inflation exceeds the expected rate of inflation. Supply may also be affected by random shocks. The OPEC oil price rises in 1973–74 and 1979–80, for example, are prime examples of negative shocks to aggregate supply.

The natural rate of growth depends on the rate of growth of the stock of capital and working population of the economy, and their productivity. Associated with growth at the natural rate is some natural rate of unemployment in the working population. Trend growth will be higher, and the natural rate of unemployment lower, the more efficiently do individual markets in the economy operate. An important determinant of efficiency in the economy is the degree of certainty with which workers and firms can plan ahead. Anything which makes planning difficult—in particular, increased variability in inflation or interest rates (or, in an open economy such as the UK, exchange rates)—will tend to reduce trend growth and raise unemployment.

If individuals and firms have perfect foresight, the natural rate of growth represents their best estimate of the trend rate of growth of their real incomes, and hence of their spending. In these circumstances, the trend rates of growth in demand and supply will be equal.

Effect of unexpected inflation

Unexpected inflation may come to affect supply in several ways. One, suggested by Friedman [1968], is as follows: Consider the expectation, held by workers and employers a year ago, about the change in prices over the coming year. Money wages will be fixed at a level which reflects that expectation. If inflation is subsequently higher than expected, firms will find profits are higher than usual, and will expand output and employment; conversely, if inflation is lower than expected, they will contract output and employment. Written as a negative relationship between unemployment and unexpected inflation, this is simply the 'inflation-augmented Phillips curve'. This is not the only rationalisation for such a relationship. Others, which do not rely on arbitrary rigidities in wages, but rather on intertemporal shifts in the supply of labour, have been developed by Lucas [1969, 1973], although much the same type of aggregate supply function emerges from these alternative theories.

A final assumption is that aggregate demand and supply should be in balance at all times. This requirement, together with the above 'surprise' supply function, has earned this type of model the label 'New Classical', rather than 'Monetarist'. An algebraic summary of the aggregate demand, supply and equilibrium conditions for this model is given in Box 1 (opposite).

The interaction of demand and supply in a single market simultaneously determines output and price in that market. The same is true in our aggregate model. Aggregate real growth and inflation are determined by the exogenous variables in the model — money supply growth, money demand growth, inflation expectations, and demand and supply shocks. Exactly what these relationships are is spelt out in Box 1. Important findings are:

- real output growth will be driven above/below trend if *either* money supply growth (relative to demand) exceeds the expected rate of inflation, *or* there are positive/negative demand or supply shocks;
- inflation will be a weighted average of *both* money supply growth (relative to demand) *and* expected inflation. In addition, demand shocks (demand-pull factors) and supply shocks (cost-push factors) can temporarily affect inflation.

It is evident that in this model growth is not an exclusively real phenomenon, nor is inflation an exclusively monetary phenomenon, as some extreme forms of monetarism argue. Instead, expectations of inflation are critical in determining the impact of monetary change on the economy.

Even so, the economists' model is clearly highly stylised, and cannot be expected to be an exact description of how the UK economy functions. But we have a good deal of evidence on the validity of the main propositions of the model, and these are not rejected, by and large, by historical data. The permanent income hypothesis, for example, has come to dominate more naïve Keynesian views of demand as dependent on current income or on the irrational whims of investors. The expectations-augmented Phillips curve has come to dominate the earlier notion that there was a stable trade-off between unemployment and actual inflation. Most

---
BOX 1: *A Minimal Monetarist Model*

The model described in the text consists of an aggregate demand function, an aggregate supply function, and an equilibrium condition. The *structural form* of the model is:

$$y^d = n + \alpha(m - p - l) + u^d \tag{1}$$

$$y^s = n + \beta(p - p^e) + u^s \tag{2}$$

$$y = y^d = y^s \tag{3}$$

Here,

y=real growth; y^d=demand growth; y^s=supply growth
n=trend or natural growth rate
m=money supply growth
p=inflation rate; p^e=expected inflation rate
l=rate of growth of demand for real money balances
u^d=demand shocks; u^s=supply shocks.

In addition, trend growth depends (negatively) on the variability of inflation, interest rates and exchange rates, as

$$n = n(\$_p, \$_r, \$_e) \tag{4}$$

Equations (1)-(4) can be solved for growth and inflation in terms of the exogenous variables of the model. The resulting *reduced form* of the model is

$$y = n(\$_p, \$_r, \$_e) + \frac{\alpha\beta}{\alpha+\beta}(m - p^e - l) + \frac{\beta}{\alpha+\beta}u^d + \frac{\alpha}{\alpha+\beta}n^s \tag{5}$$

$$p = \frac{\alpha}{\alpha+\beta}(m - l) + \frac{\beta}{\alpha+\beta}p^e + \frac{1}{\alpha+\beta}(u^d - u^s) \tag{6}$$

---

disputation concerns the rate at which equilibrium is established between aggregate demand and supply. A readable critique of the New Classical model in the UK along these lines is provided by Davies [1985], and by much of the evidence submitted to the inquiry by the Treasury and Civil Service Committee [1980-81] which followed the publication of the MTFS.

At worst, this evidence suggests that the above propositions about growth and inflation may be valid in the long run rather than the short, an interpretation which does not affect any of the arguments I want to develop below and with which I would not disagree. I therefore intend to maintain this model, and discuss whether, within the theory of economic policy implicit in the model, UK policy in the years 1980-86 has been well conceived. Some basic criticisms of the model, most notably the question of the stability of money demand and the omission of short-run interest-rate and exchange-rate dynamics, will be raised in the course of the discussion.

III. MONETARY TARGETS: THE INDICATOR
PROBLEM

Monetary policy in the framework outlined above has three components. It is clearly necessary to reduce money growth in order to reduce the rate of inflation. But it is also desirable to reduce inflationary expectations, in order to reduce inflation itself and to boost income growth. And it is desirable that money growth and expectations be controlled in a way which imposes least costs on the real economy in terms of uncertainty about inflation, interest rates and exchange rates.

Types of Monetary Targets

As a result, monetary targets have three distinct roles to play in the implementation of such a policy.

First, a monetary aggregate may be used as an *operating target* since the monetary authorities do not have the means to control money growth directly. The authorities can sell debt only through operations in the open market, and hope that this brings about the desired contraction in the money stock. In these circumstances, the authorities will find it useful to have some operating target for a variable which does indicate the likely direction and size of the impact of open-market operations on the money stock. This target might be a quantity, such as the monetary base, or a price, such as an interest rate or an exchange rate. Such a target must by definition be under the indirect control of the authorities. Which target is chosen, we shall later argue, depends on what distribution of uncertainty is considered optimal by the authorities. Irrespective of this choice, the function of any operating target is to convey, within a short period, information to the authorities about the net impact of their past actions on monetary conditions.

The *second* role for a monetary target is to act as an *indicator* of future inflation, a focus for inflation expectations. Since, in our monetarist model, money affects inflation and output, advance warning of monetary changes can help avoid costly errors in expectations and reduce uncertainty about inflation. One criterion for selecting such an indicator is that it must be a good predictor of inflation. Another is that its relationship with future inflation must be simple enough to be understood by individuals and firms. Some monetary aggregate is an obvious choice for such a role. Yet, irrespective of what aggregate is chosen, the function of the indicator is to convey to the general public information about the future medium- to long-term trend in inflation.

The *third* use of a monetary target is as an *insulator* of aggregate prices against political pressure to reflate. Because unexpected inflation raises growth of output, there is liable to be chronic political pressure to reflate from governments seeking popularity by temporarily raising voters' incomes. This possibility means that there is liable to be high uncertainty about inflation, particularly in advance of elections. The announcement of a monetary target represents a commitment by the authorities not to be influenced by such short-term pressures, and should reduce uncertainty about inflation, and hence improve the performance of the real economy. The insulator aggregate must be under the control of the government, and so the insulator aggregate might be the same as the operating target. What matters more than the precise choice of aggregate, however, is that such targets are published for a number of years ahead, and that these targets are respected as constraints on the actions of the monetary authorities.

The distinction between operating targets and indicators is well-established in economic theory. Saving [1967] and Burger [1971] provide very clear accounts of their use in implementing monetary policy under uncertainty. The insulator role of monetary targets is also well-established, in the sense that such targets form a key part of the 'monetary constitution' advocated by Buchanan and Wagner [1977] and others as a means of depoliticising monetary policy.

Yet these distinctions have not been clearly made in the targets set in the MTFS. The targeted monetary aggregate, initially £M3, is loosely referred to as an 'intermediate target'. On the one hand, it is clearly intended to act as an indicator of inflationary trends. Thus

> 'The speed with which inflation falls will depend invariably on expectations ... It is to provide a firm basis for those expectations that the Government has announced its firm commitment to a progressive reduction in money growth'.[1]

On the other hand, the Treasury has repeatedly emphasised the controllability of the 'intermediate target' as a criterion for first

---

[1] *Financial Statement and Budget Report, 1980-1*, HC 500, HMSO, Part 2, p. 16.

selecting, and subsequently dropping, £M3. This suggests that £M3 was also viewed as an operating target. Certainly, in the early days of the MTFS, the financial markets treated £M3 announcements in this way, with overshoots in the aggregate inducing expectations of a corrective tightening of monetary policy. It is technically possible for a single variable to act both as indicator and operating target, but this would constitute rather a special case. We argue below that the conflation of the two concepts has led to an unnecessary degree of confusion, and a loss of credibility, in the MTFS.

The remainder of this section is devoted to an analysis of the MTFS targets as indicators. We take up the separate question of what operating target can best control money growth in the following section.

Indicator Policy, 1980-86

If the monetary targets in the MTFS had been successful as indicators of future inflation, we would expect to observe a particular profile of growth and inflation over the period 1980-86. If they have been unsuccessful, we would expect to observe quite a different pattern.

In the absence of a credible indicator, an unexpected monetary deflation of, say, 10 per cent relative to money demand will reduce inflation, according to our earlier theory, by some fraction of that 10 per cent. Since this inflation rate will be lower than expected, growth in output will also be driven below its natural rate. In time, inflation expectations will presumably adapt to the lower inflation rate, reducing the actual inflation rate further, but also reducing the gap between actual and trend growth. Eventually, when expected inflation has fallen by 10 per cent, the actual rate of inflation will be correctly anticipated, and growth will resume its trend path. Monetary deflation without a credible indicator will thus reduce inflation only slowly, and will be accompanied by short-term real costs in the form of below-trend output.

If a credible indicator target is published simultaneously with the monetary deflation, actual inflation will fall faster and there will be no short-term real costs. The target ensures that inflation expectations will fall in line with money growth, rather than lagging behind it. This reinforces the impact of lower money growth on inflation; and it ensures that perceived real balances do not fall

---

BOX 2: *Monetary Indicators and Rational Expectations*

As suggested by Muth [1961], it is plausible to think of the inflation expectations p^e in our model being formed in a manner consistent with the predictions of the model.

Equation (6) in Box 1 (page 61) suggests that inflation depends on money supply and demand growth, on inflation expectations themselves, and on unpredictable shocks to aggregate demand and supply. The best that an individual could do would therefore be to frame probability distributions for the growth of money supply m and money demand growth I, and solve for p^e in terms of the statistical expected values of these variables. For simplicity, assume that money demand growth is known with certainty, but that individuals' pdf for money supply growth is

$$m = m^e + u^m \tag{7}$$

where u^m is a zero-mean disturbance term. Then a rational expectation of inflation is, from (6)

$$p^e = m^{e-l} \tag{8}$$

and hence

$$y = n + \frac{\alpha\beta}{\alpha+\beta}(m-m^e) + \frac{\beta}{\alpha+\beta}u^d + \frac{\alpha}{\alpha+\beta}u^s \tag{9}$$

$$p = (m-l) - \frac{\beta}{\alpha+\beta}(m-m^e) + \frac{1}{\alpha+\beta}(u^d - u^s) \tag{10}$$

Suppose also that the authorities can control money growth along its target path m^t subject to some zero-mean control error u^t, as

$$m = m^t + u^t \tag{11}$$

If the monetary target m^t is announced, then $m^e = m^t$ and the only impact of monetary policy on deviations of growth and inflation from trend will arise from these control errors, since $m - m^e = m - m^t = u^t$ in (9) and (10). However, if the monetary target is not announced, $m^e = m^t + u^e$, say, when u^e is the error in the public's estimate of the authorities' intentions. In this case, $m - m^e = u^t - u^e$, so that the variability of growth and inflation is increased.

---

relative to money demand. The result is to reduce the variability of both growth and inflation around trend, as demonstrated in Box 2.

The behaviour of inflation and growth of output in the UK in the years following the publication of the MTFS is summarised in Table 1. The figures clearly more closely resemble those predicted to result from a deflation without the benefit of a credible monetary indicator. Real growth fell well below trend in 1980 and 1981, and inflation declined only gradually from its 1980 peak and stabilised around 5 per cent in 1984. This impression is reinforced by the figures for inflation expectations over this period reported in column 5 of the Table. Inflation expectations have been persistently higher than actual inflation since 1980, and decline only after the

TABLE 1
UK ECONOMIC PERFORMANCE, 1979-86 (%)

Financial Year	Real Growth[a]	Inflation[b]	Money Base	Growth £M3	Inflation Expectations[c]	Real Exchange Rate[d]
	(1)	(2)	(3)	(4)	(5)	(6)
1979/80	2.3	12.8	7.7	12.6	19.1	18.8
1980/81	−2.9	14.9	6.6	19.9	12.7	12.3
1981/82	−0.9	5.9	5.0	13.4	11.1	−9.6
1982/83	2.3	7.7	5.6	10.1	5.0	−10.8
1983/84	2.8	4.9	5.5	10.2	5.1	3.1
1984/85	1.7	5.1	4.2	10.0	5.5	−9.4
1985/86	3.6	4.1	5.4	17.0	4.9	8.9

[a] Gross domestic product at factor cost, in 1980 prices.
[b] GDP deflator, per cent change through year.
[c] Gallup Poll, at beginning of year.
[d] Change in sterling exchange rate, adjusted for relative producer price inflation.

actual rate of inflation has declined. This suggests an adaptive response to errors. It does not suggest that the public gave immediate credence to the MTFS targets in 1980, nor to the targets announced in subsequent budgets.

These expectations data come from Gallup Poll surveys, and represent the average expectations of the public at large (Batchelor and Orr [forthcoming]). But wage inflation over this period has also persistently run ahead of inflation, by more than growth of productivity, which suggests that similar expectations were also held by key participants in wage negotiations.

One reason for the lack of credibility in the authorities' intentions towards inflation is apparent from column 4 of Table 1 which sets out the growth rates of the target aggregate, £M3, over the period. In the MTFS of March 1980, growth of £M3 was projected to decelerate from the range 7-11 per cent in 1980-81, to around 4-8 per cent in 1983-84. In fact, growth of £M3 was over 12 per cent in 1980-81, and has remained in double figures ever since, actually *rising* in 1985-86. Over the period of operation of the MTFS, £M3 has ceased to be helpful as a monetary indicator, in the sense that it has not constituted a simple predictor for subsequent movements of inflation.

A second reason for the lack of credibility about the authorities' intentions was their reaction to the early signs of breakdown in the £M3 indicator. In successive budgets after 1980, the Chancellor introduced, alongside the £M3 target, a succession of additional indicators also intended to act as predictors of inflation. The £M3 target range was overshot in 1981 principally because of the return of deposits to the banking system following the abolition of the Supplementary Special Deposit (SSD) Scheme ('the Corset'). Because these deposits had migrated outside the banking system, in the 1981 Budget a slightly broader aggregate, PSL1 (Private Sector Liquidity 1, which includes wholesale non-bank deposits), was briefly canvassed as a superior monetary indicator. In the 1982-83 Budget, persistent differences between narrow and broad monetary aggregates led to a common target range being specified across the whole spectrum of definitions of the money supply, with M1 at the narrow end and PSL2 (PSL1 *plus* building society deposits) at the broad end. In addition, it was noted that

> 'The behaviour of the exchange rate can help in the interpretation of monetary conditions, particularly when the different aggregates are known to be distorted',

and that

> 'despite the relatively rapid growth in broad money, the balance of the evidence suggests that, as intended, financial conditions have been moderately restrictive during the past year. This is supported by the growth in narrow money and the performance of money GDP'.[2]

Two new indicators—the exchange rate and money GDP—were therefore added to the arsenal. The 1983-84 Budget continued the practice of stipulating a common target range for all aggregates. By 1984-85, however, the narrow aggregate M1 was also growing too rapidly because of the growing practice of paying interest on demand deposits; and the response of the authorities was to suggest that an even narrower measure of money, the monetary base M0, might be a better indicator. Separate targets were set for M0 and £M3. In addition, since it was deemed desirable to target an aggregate which represented balances held for transactions pur-

---

[2] *Financial Statement and Budget Report 1982–3*, HC237, Session 1981–82, HMSO, 1982, p. 14.

poses, rather than simply for the interest they bore, a new aggregate, labelled M2, was created, consisting of cash and liquid balances at banks and other financial institutions. In the event, M2 rose more rapidly than either M0 or £M3 and so was dropped in the 1985-86 Budget. In the 1986-87 Budget, the £M3 target was also dropped completely. A range was set for base growth, with a rider that the rate of growth of money GDP would be used as a check on whether policy is tight or lax.

The very profusion of these indicators, and the obvious disarray of official thinking on the problem, is perhaps sufficient explanation of why the public chose to forecast inflation not on the basis of government promises about the future, but on the basis of their (steadily improving) track record.

The Problem of £M3

These experiences with monetary indicators since 1980 lead to three questions. Is the above interpretation of the 1980-81 recession as the product of an unexpected monetary deflation correct? Why precisely has the £M3 target broken down? Can a new indicator variable be found?

While the behaviour of £M3 in the early 1980s suggests that monetary policy was not deflationary, the behaviour of other aggregates, including the narrow monetary base shown in Table 1 (column 3), suggests that it was. A proximate cause of the fall in output in manufacturing was undoubtedly the sharp rise in sterling, from an effective rate of 81.5 in 1978 to 96.1 in 1980, and this has been interpreted, by Niehans [1981] and Buiter and Miller [1982], for example, as an instance of the tendency of exchange rates to overshoot their equilibrium values in response to a sharp change in the monetary environment.

Other explanations of the recession in output and the appreciation in the exchange rate are possible. It was the substantial building-up of stocks of 1978-79, for example, which was the reason that, although final demand actually rose in 1980-81, demand was met from stocks rather than from current production. The appreciation of sterling clearly owed something to the increase in UK oil production, and the oil price rise of 1979-80, as argued by Forsyth and Kay [1980] and Aliber [1984]; and proponents of the overshooting arguments have found it difficult to explain the later violent depreciation of sterling in 1983 (*cf.*, for example, Buiter and Miller [1983]). But it is hard to argue with the proposition that monetary tightness played *some* part in the problems of the real economy in 1980-81.

The history of £M3 relative to inflation is shown in the top panel of Figure 1. The reason for its choice in 1980 as an indicator is plain. The peaks in £M3 growth in 1967-68, 1973 and 1978, and its troughs in 1969-70, were followed—after a lag of around two years—by similar peaks and troughs in inflation. Its breakdown after 1980 is also plain in the contrast between the persistently high rate of £M3 growth and the low rate of inflation.

Three reasons have been advanced for this apparently perverse behaviour. Two concern changes in the supply of money. First, the ending of the Supplementary Special Deposit (SSD) Scheme in July 1980, a constraint on the growth of banks' interest-bearing liabilities, led to a return of many 'disintermediated' funds which had been held temporarily outside the banking system during the period of operation of the scheme. To the extent that the rapid growth in £M3 in 1980-81 was due to re-intermediation, it had no implications for inflation; money growth which had previously been concealed was simply being brought out into the open.

Second, the ending of the SSD scheme also marked the beginning of a period of intense competition among banks, and between banks and other financial institutions. One aspect of this increased competition was more active liability management. Time deposits at banks paid more competitive interest rates; and, most striking of all, a growing proportion of demand deposits paid interest to holders. As a result, an increasing proportion of £M3 balances was held as assets, rather than for transactions purposes. To the extent that subsequent growth in £M3 represented the accumulation of assets which the public intended to hold rather than spend, it also had no implication for output and inflation.

The third difficulty with £M3 is related to the demand for it. The fall in inflation expectations which eventually followed the MTFS will tend to make more attractive that part of £M3 which does not pay a competitive rate of interest. In other words, demand for £M3 will grow faster if an anticipated monetary deflation is in train. In these circumstances, a small fall in money growth may induce a large fall in the gap between growth in the supply and demand for money; and, as we have seen, it is the size of this gap which is

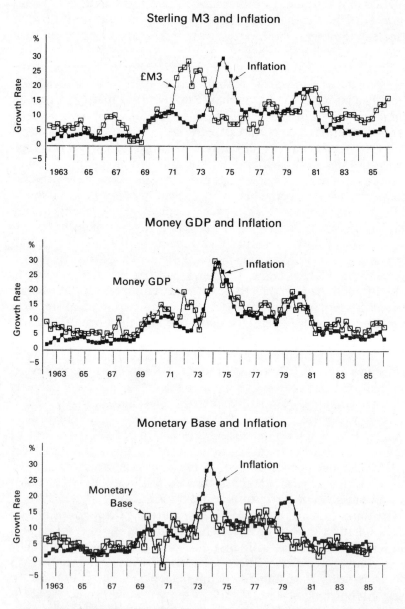

Figure 1: Inflation and Monetary Indicators, 1963–86, Quarterly
(*per cent change on year earlier*)

important for determining the impact of monetary policy on the economy. Thus, £M3 growth might be quite high, but still be deflationary, because the demand for it has been raised by the fall in inflation expectations. This case is made by Budd and Holly [1986], who show that over a long period there is a strong inverse relationship between changes in inflation and £M3 growth. Of course, as inflation expectations stabilise, so also should demand for money; so a corollary of this argument is that it is important that, after this transitional period of high demand growth, the money supply should be cut back in line with the long-term inflation target.

A number of alternatives to £M3 as a monetary target have been canvassed, and all have been adopted at one time or another by the Government (above) in its attempts to influence inflation expectations. The principle of seeking an alternative monetary indicator is a sound one; what is unsound is the frequency with which the Government has switched from one aggregate to another.

The criterion for an ideal monetary indicator is that it should bear a stable and a simple relationship to future movements in aggregate prices. Empirical investigation and *a priori* reasoning can help decide what aggregate might best fulfil this function in the environment of the mid-1980s.

Several of the indicators used by the UK authorities are clear non-runners on such grounds. Money GDP, for example, is as much an objective of policy as an indicator. The notion that changes in money GDP might lead to changes in inflation seems to stem from early Federal Reserve Bank of St Louis studies of the impact of monetary policy, which showed an immediate effect of monetary deflation on nominal income, initially in the form of a fall in real output, but subsequently in the form of a fall in the rate of inflation. As the middle panel of Figure 1 shows, however, changes in nominal income have more or less coincided with changes in inflation in the UK. The use of the exchange rate as an indicator seems equally misguided. The exchange rate is a candidate for the role of operating target, but not of monetary indicator. As I have argued, an appreciation of the exchange rate may signal a monetary shock or a real shock (such as an oil price rise). Similarly, it may signal an improvement in the domestic economy or a deterioration in the rest of the world. Too many extraneous factors influence the exchange rate to make it helpful in forecasting inflation.

71

Predictive power of £M3

A large number of empirical tests have been conducted on whether narrow aggregates, such as the monetary base or M1, or broad aggregates, such as £M3, can best predict inflation. These studies uniformly favour £M3. The superiority of £M3 over the monetary base as a predictor of inflation is obvious from a comparison of the top and bottom panels of Figure 1; movements in the base are virtually contemporaneous with movements in inflation. This is confirmed by more formal tests. For example, Holly and Longbottom [1982] find that movements in £M3 are typically followed by proportionate movements in aggregate prices, although with a long—$3\frac{1}{2}$- to 4-year—lag; somewhat reluctantly, Parkin and Bade [1984] reach the same conclusion that changes in £M3 growth systematically precede changes in inflation, but this is not true of the monetary base or M1. Mills [1983] finds similarly, in an assessment of the predictive power of various monetary aggregates, about inflation and nominal income growth, that

> 'restricting attention to anything less than the broadest monetary aggregate currently available involves a considerable amount of information loss' (p.39).

In other words, £M3 is demonstrably the best predictor of inflation. The difficulty is that its relationship with inflation is not sufficiently *simple* for it to serve as a focus for expectations.

These historical studies do not meet the criticism that the *structure* of £M3 has changed irrevocably since 1980, and so cannot be counted on to maintain a stable relationship with inflation in the future. Evidence on the past stability of money demand, or its predictive power, is of no value in choosing an indicator in such circumstances. The choice must be made on *a priori* grounds, which is why some commentators have been led to argue for the use of a very narrow aggregate, such as the monetary base, or non-interest-bearing M1.

The principle of these arguments is a good one. It is that money may be held for transactions and savings purposes. In the pre-1980 days of uncompetitive banking it was safe to assume that any bank deposit was intended to be used for transactions at some time or another, since—in view of its low rate of return—there was no other reason to hold it. Since 1980, with many deposits paying competitive rates of interest, it is safe to assume only that cash and non-interest-earning current accounts will be spent on goods. The closer correlation between base growth and inflation since 1980 provides some empirical support for this argument.

But it can be pushed too far. Even if money earns a competitive interest rate, it can be used as a 'temporary abode of purchasing power'. An ideal procedure, as discussed by Barnett [1980] and Spindt [1985], is to weight each type of deposit by a factor reflecting the probability of its being traded for goods or bonds. The probability of time-deposits and interest-bearing demand deposits being spent has clearly declined, but has not vanished, in recent years. Use of the monetary base or non-interest-bearing M1 as indicators is less than ideal, therefore, since they assign zero weights to interest-bearing types of money. Yet, given the practical problems of introducing the public to some new ideal 'index of monetary services', with weights which change from year to year as bank behaviour changes, perhaps the use of one such narrow aggregate represents the best compromise now available.

IV. MONETARY CONTROLS: THE PROBLEM OF THE OPERATING TARGET

Any attempt at monetary restraint is liable to be jeopardised if no mechanisms exist to control and monitor the impact of policy on the rate of growth of the money stock. To its credit, the Thatcher Government, in parallel with the launching of the MTFS, initiated a debate on monetary control procedures, and the value of using the monetary base rather than an interest rate as the operating target. Alongside this debate, argument has continued over the value to the UK of participating fully in the exchange-rate mechanism of the EMS. This would effectively mean using movements in the European Currency Unit (ECU) exchange rate, rather than any interest rate or the monetary base, as an operating target to trigger open-market operations. The outcome has been an official discussion document on *Monetary Control* (HM Treasury and Bank of England [1980]); a new compromise framework for short-term operating procedures which targets the monetary base, unless interest rates stray outside an unspecified, moving, target band

(Bank of England [1981]); and a series of inquiries into the functioning of the EMS (House of Lords, Select Committee on the European Communities [1983]; House of Commons, Treasury and Civil Service Committee [1985]), which are generally favourable to the principle of UK membership.

This section examines, first, the framework of official monetary analysis, and, secondly, considerations governing the choice of an operating target.

Official Monetary Analysis: Money *v.* Credit

Most monetary economics textbooks develop a simple framework for the analysis of the supply of money, centred on the idea that the money stock is built on the supply of 'base money'—cash plus bank deposits at the Bank of England—provided by the monetary authorities. The banking system can create a volume of deposits on the back of this stock of base money, to a degree which is limited only by the prudence of the banks in holding cash reserves, and the reluctance of the general public to re-deposit cash with the banks. The money stock, M, is the sum of cash in the hands of the public, C, and bank deposits, D; the base is the sum of C and bank reserves R. On any definition of money, it is possible to write the stock M as the product of the base, B, and a 'money multiplier', K (so that money, M, equals K times B). Moreover, the size of this money multiplier depends on the ratio of cash to deposits held by the public, and the ratio of reserves to deposits held by the banks. The more cash or reserves held, the less money (in the wider sense) created by the multiplier process of money and credit.

Similarly, the growth in the money stock can be broken down into two parts—the growth in the multiplier and the growth in the base; and any growth in the multiplier can in turn be traced to movements in the cash and reserve ratios. The virtue of this particular analysis is that it helps the authorities see clearly how much of any monetary change is ascribable to their own actions, in changing B, the 'monetary base'; how much to the actions of the public, in changing the cash to deposit ratio, C/D; and how much to the actions of the banks, in changing their reserves to deposits ratio, R/D.

It is important to emphasise that the usefulness of this base-multiplier approach to money-supply analysis is quite independent of whether the authorities choose to use the base B as an operating target. It is equally useful under both base and interest-rate targeting procedures.

The official approach to money-supply analysis is built around quite another identity. A little juggling (Batchelor [1983]) with the balance sheets of the banking sector and the monetary authorities reveals that (ignoring changes in the liabilities of banks other than deposits) the following logically holds, as an identity:

> The change in Sterling M3 EQUALS the PSBR *plus* the change in Reserves *plus* lending to the public by the banking sector (including the Bank of England) *minus* sales of government debt to the public outside the banks.

This identity holds a fascination for the monetary authorities because it shows linkages between monetary growth and fiscal policy, balance-of-payments policy, debt policy and credit policy. It is cited by John Fforde [1983] as a reason for the choice of £M3 as the MTFS target; and it is the source of the now notorious statement which begins the 1980 Green Paper on *Monetary Control* (HM Treasury and Bank of England [1980]):

> 'There are a number of policy instruments available to the authorities in influencing monetary conditions. Of these, the main ones are fiscal policy, debt management, administered changes in short-term interest rates, direct controls on the financial system, and operations in the foreign exchange market'.

The first problem with this counterpart asset approach to money-stock analysis is that it is quite possible to describe changes in *any* money-stock definition in this fashion. In particular,

> the change in the base simply EQUALS the PSBR *plus* the change in Reserves *plus* the Bank of England's lending to the public *minus* sales of government debt to the public and the commercial banks.

The second, and more profound, problem with the counterpart asset approach is that it reflects a preoccupation with credit rather than money. Clearly, both of the above expressions are identities, and both are equally true; but the base identity is much more helpful than the £M3 identity in understanding monetary change. The base identity allows changes in the money stock to be broken down into distinct components, reflecting the distinct contributions of the authorities, the public, and the banks to monetary growth. In contrast, the counterpart asset identity is confusing in two respects. New loans from the Bank of England are treated on the same footing as loans by commercial banks. But only the first will, other things equal, increase the money stock; the second will be important only if the reserve ratio changes. Similarly, government debt sales to the non-bank private sector are treated by the identity as qualitatively different from debt sales to banks. But *any* debt sale will, other things equal, reduce the size of the base, and hence contract the money stock. These anomalies begin to make sense only if the identity is regarded as a basis for analysing *credit*. In this case all loans do have the same effect, in increasing credit; and debt sales to the non-bank public do indeed have a special status, in that only they contract private-sector liquidity.

The perseverance of the Treasury and the Bank of England with this 'counterpart asset' approach to monetary analysis is not, therefore, a harmless bit of fun with balance-sheet identities. It reinforces a pre-monetarist view of the importance of credit in the economy, and has led to an excessive preoccupation by the Bank of England with commercial bank lending, when it might have been better engaged in analysing its own contribution to money growth, and the determinants of change in the money multiplier.

Interest Targeting *v.* Monetary Base Control

It is straightforward to analyse the main issues concerning the choice of an operating target, within the base-multiplier framework. I shall examine, first, the differing properties of an interest-targeting regime and a base-targeting regime, and, second, the question of whether an exchange-rate target would be better still.

If the authorities had complete control over the money supply, and perfect information about the demand for money, there would be little to choose between base and interest targeting. Either could be guaranteed to deliver the desired rate of money growth. The choice becomes critical only because money demand and supply are not known with certainty.

Under interest targeting, interest-rate uncertainty is reduced to zero. But every fluctuation in money demand at this interest rate must be accommodated by a fluctuation in money supply, so that monetary uncertainty is high. Moreover, pinning down an interest rate is not sufficient to pin down the inflation rate, as demonstrated in Box 3 (below).

Under base control, monetary uncertainty is lower than under interest targeting, but is not reduced to zero. Although the authorities may adhere strictly to their base target, changes in the portfolio behaviour of banks and the general public will, by changing the money multiplier, cause the money supply to fluctuate. These movements, and any fluctuations in money demand, also cause the interest rate to fluctuate. The analytics of this are also set out in Box 3.

As a result, fixing interest rates allows money (and so prices) to vary, whereas fixing money holds prices fixed but allows interest rates to vary in response to shocks to money supply and demand.

BOX 3: *Interest Rate Targets* v. *Monetary Base Control*

The discussion in the text assumes the following demand and supply conditions in the money market:

$$m^d = p+n-\gamma r+v^d \qquad (12)$$

$$m^s = b+k+\delta r+v^s \qquad (13)$$

$$m = m^d = m^s \qquad (14)$$

Here,

m=monetary growth; m^d=money demand growth; m^s=money supply growth
p=inflation
n=trend or natural growth rate
r=change in nominal interest rate
b=monetary base growth
k=trend growth in money multiplier
v^d=money demand shocks; v^s=money supply shocks
   Under interest targeting,

$$r=0 \qquad (15)$$
$$m=p+n+v^d \qquad (16)$$

Hence the variance of interest rates is zero, and the variance of m stems entirely from demand shocks. Substitution of (16) into (10) confirms that inflation is indeterminate under this type of monetary régime.
   Under base targeting, $b=b^t$, say, and the reduced form for r and m is

$$r=\frac{1}{\gamma+\delta}(p+n-k-b^t)+\frac{1}{\gamma+\delta}(v^d-v^s) \qquad (17)$$

$$m=\frac{\delta}{\gamma+\delta}(p+n)+\frac{\delta}{\gamma+\delta}(k+b^e)+\frac{\delta}{\gamma+\delta}v^d+\frac{\gamma}{\gamma+\delta}v^s \qquad (18)$$

The variance of m is less in (18) than in (16), but the variance of r is obviously greater in (17) than in (15).

The choice between interest-rate targeting and a base control technique thus depends on (*a*) the seriousness with which the indeterminacy under interest targeting is viewed, and (*b*) whether uncertainty about interest rates or about inflation is more damaging to the economy, in terms of its impact on the underlying ('natural') growth rate generated by supply-side factors.

Unfortunately, these are not the terms in which the debate on monetary control has been conducted. To be sure, the trade-off between interest-rate variability and monetary (inflation) variability is well understood. But the compelling reason given in the Green Paper and the earlier Bank of England (1979) analysis for eschewing monetary base control is the notion that its implementation involves 'withdrawing the lender of last resort function' of the Bank of England (Cmnd. 7858 [1980], p. 9). This seems an entirely specious objection. It is true that under a base-targeting system the Bank could not meet daily cash 'shortages' in the banking system; the banks would instead be obliged to hold higher reserves. But this is hardly an exercise of last-resort lending as envisaged by Bagehot, who stipulated that the Bank of England should lend without limit at a penal rate in this last resort.

Exchange-Rate Targeting: The EMS

A decision to peg the sterling exchange rate is a decision to use this exchange-rate target as the operating target for monetary policy, expanding the base when the exchange rate appreciates relative to its central parity, contracting it when the exchange rate threatens to appreciate. These changes in the money supply will also cause interest rates to change. The benefits from an exchange-rate operating target, such as would be entailed by full EMS membership, lie in any external monetary discipline which the target might impose, and in the reduction of exchange-rate uncertainty. The costs accrue in the form of interest-rate and monetary uncertainty.

In 1978-79, when UK membership of the EMS was first mooted, the case in favour of membership was that it would effectively entail UK monetary policy being run by the Bundesbank. The case against was that this was a second-best alternative to the imposition of monetary discipline by the Treasury itself. The success of the MTFS has made the argument for external discipline redundant. So is the exchange-rate uncertainty experienced under the present regime of floating rates more damaging than the alternatives of interest-rate or monetary uncertainty?

Because of the peculiar vulnerability of the UK to oil-price shocks, this trade-off is probably significant. Unlike that between interest-rate and monetary uncertainty, it seems possible to deliver some judgement on whether it would be desirable to reduce exchange-rate uncertainty. The reason is that exchange risks fall specifically on one part of the economy, the tradeable goods sector, while interest-rate and monetary uncertainty have effects which are widely distributed across the general public. This means, of course, that there is a more coherent pressure group, centred on the CBI, calling for a stabilisation of exchange rates, than there is calling for interest-rate or monetary stabilisation. The relevant question, however, is: Which of the affected groups in the economy is best able to diversify away the risks it faces under the alternative operating rules which the authorities might follow? In this respect, the tradeable goods sector is in an advantageous position. There are well developed forward markets in which exchange-rate risk can be hedged. But the general public is at a disadvantage. Although some mechanisms exist for handling interest-rate and price (inflation) risk, such as indexation, these devices are relatively underdeveloped.

Since a private market exists which can provide insurance against exchange risk, but no such market exists to insure against monetary risk, there would seem to be a better case for government provision of monetary stability than of the exchange-rate stability which is promised by full EMS membership.

As with the debate on interest targeting and base control, the terms on which EMS membership has been rejected have not necessarily been those which the above theory points to as most relevant. For example, the Treasury and Civil Service Committee [1985] notes that 'The problem of misalignment is more crucial than that of fluctuation' (p. xxii). The committee's main reason for not recommending UK entry into the EMS was that the prevailing exchange rates did not offer UK exporters a competitive advantage. This was echoed in the Government's subsequent comment that the UK would join the EMS when the time was ripe.

V. CONCLUDING COMMENTS

The main lesson I would draw from this examination of the recent debates on UK monetary policy is that, while it may be hard to change entrenched inflation expectations, it is harder still to shift entrenched intellectual positions. On all of the critical problems which have confronted policy-makers—the choice of an indicator, the choice of an operating target—economic theory has strong statements to make on what the appropriate criteria are for these choices. In the case of the indicator, predictive power must be traded off against complexity. In the case of the operating target, inflation uncertainty must be traded off against interest-rate or exchange-rate uncertainty.

Yet, in addressing all these problems, policy-makers appear to have been hampered by an unwillingness to conduct their arguments in these terms. Instead, they have brought to the problems a set of principles which is either confused (in the case of indicators), outdated (monetary control), or political rather than economic in nature (the EMS). Perhaps it is enough that the Government, and the country, has embraced the big idea—of the Medium-Term Financial Strategy. On the other hand, perhaps we could expect more.

REFERENCES AND RELATED READINGS

Aliber, R. Z. [1984]: 'Structural Change, Monetary Policy, and the Foreign Exchange Value of Sterling', in B. Griffiths and G. E. Wood (eds.), *Monetarism in the United Kingdom* (Macmillan, London).

Bank of England [1981]: 'Monetary Control: Next Steps', *Quarterly Bulletin*, March.

Barnett, W. A. [1980]: 'Economic Monetary Aggregation: An Application of Index Number and Aggregation Theory', *Journal of Econometrics*.

Batchelor, R. A. [1983]: 'What is Wrong with Official Money Supply Analysis?', *City University Business School Economic Review*, 1.

Batchelor, R. A. and A. B. Orr [forthcoming]: 'Inflation Expectations Revisited', *Economica*.

Beenstock, M. [1980]: *A Neoclassical Analysis of Macroeconomic Policy* (Cambridge University Press).

Buchanan, J. M. and R. E. Wagner [1977]: *Democracy in Deficit: the Political Legacy of Lord Keynes* (Academic Press, London).

Budd, A. and S. Holly [1986]: 'Does Broad Money Matter?', *Economic Outlook*, July.

Buiter, W. and M. H. Miller [1982]: 'Real Exchange Rate Overshooting and the Output Cost of Bringing down Inflation', *European Economic Review*.

Buiter, W. and M. H. Miller [1983]: 'Changing the Rules: the Economic Consequences of the Thatcher Regime', *Brookings Papers in Economic Activity*, 2.

Burger, A. E. [1971]: 'The Implementation Problem of Monetary Policy', *Federal Reserve Bank of St Louis Review*, March.

Davies, G. [1985]: *Governments Can Affect Unemployment*, Employment Institute, London.

Fforde, J. S. [1983]: 'Setting Monetary Objectives', *Bank of England Quarterly Bulletin*, June.

Foot, M. D. K. W., C. A. E. Goodhart and A. C. Hotson [1979]: 'Monetary Base Control', *Bank of England Quarterly Bulletin*, June.

Forsyth, P. J. and J. A. Kay [1980]: 'The Economic Implications of North Sea Oil Reserves', *Fiscal Studies*, 1.

Friedman, M. [1968]: 'The Role of Monetary Policy', *American Economic Review*.

HM Treasury and Bank of England [1980]: *Monetary Control* (Cmnd. 7858, HMSO).

Holly, S. and J. A. Longbottom [1982]: 'The Empirical Relationship between the Money Stock and the Price Level in the United Kingdom; A Test of Causality', *Bulletin of Economic Research*, 34 (1).

House of Lords, Select Committee on the European Communities [1983]: *European Monetary System* (HMSO).

Lucas, R. E. Jnr. [1973]: 'Some International Evidence on Output-Inflation Tradeoffs', *American Economic Review*, 63.

Lucas, R. E. Jnr. and L. A. Rapping [1969]: 'Real Wages, Employment and Inflation', *Journal of Political Economy*, 77.

Mills, T. C. [1983]: 'The Information Content of the UK Monetary Components and Aggregates', *Bulletin of Economic Research*, 35 (1).

Muth, J. F. [1961]: 'Rational Expectations and the Theory of Price Movements', *Econometrica*.

Niehans, J. [1981]: *The Appreciation of Sterling—Causes, Effects, Policies* (Centre for Policy Studies, London).

Parkin, M. and R. Bade [1984]: 'Is Sterling M3 the Right Aggregate?', in B. Griffiths and G. E. Wood, *Monetarism in the United Kingdom* (Macmillan, London).

Sargent, T. J. and N. Wallace [1985]: 'Rational Expectations, the Optimal Monetary Instrument, and the Optional Money Supply Rule', *Journal of Political Economy*, 83.

Saving, T. R. [1967]: 'Monetary Policy Targets and Indicators', *Journal of Political Economy*.

Spindt, P. A. [1985]: 'Money Is What Money Does: Monetary Aggregation and the Equation of Exchange', *Journal of Political Economy*.

Treasury and Civil Service Committee [1980]: *Memoranda on Monetary Policy* (HMSO).

Treasury and Civil Service Committee [1981]: *Monetary Policy* (HMSO).

Treasury and Civil Service Committee [1985]: *The Financial and Economic Consequences of UK Membership of the European Communities: The European Monetary System* (HMSO).

Commentary—1
C. A. E. GOODHART
London School of Economics

Roy Batchelor begins by setting out a basic monetarist model, whose validity he assumes rather than justifies. Against that background he then discusses the selection of monetary targets, both on theoretical grounds and in the light of recent developments, notably the breakdown of the previous econometric relationship, whereby £M3 appeared to have a stable lead relationship with nominal incomes. He then turns once more to the old battlefield of monetary base control, and ends with a short discussion of the arguments for and against entry into the exchange rate mechanism of the EMS. I find it hard to work up much enthusiasm for returning to the monetary base argument yet again. We have all gone over that ground so often, and the positions taken by the various participants in that discussion are so well known. I can only agree with his statement that 'while it may be hard to change entrenched inflation expectations, it is harder still to shift entrenched intellectual positions'. And, alas, I see no great likelihood of shifting *his* entrenched position.

In some part our differing positions on this and other economic issues may be related to a difference in our fundamental views about the working of the economy as a whole. Indeed, I thought it sensible that Batchelor did not attempt to try to justify his monetarist model of the UK economy, since I do not believe that it can be effectively justified. Thus he states that

> 'The basic assumption of the monetarist model is that the total activity in the economy, and aggregate prices, are determined in the same way as quantities and prices in individual markets, by the interaction of demand and supply' (p. 58).

Thus he clearly believes that most markets work efficiently with price changes occurring rapidly to equate demand and supply. I do not. While I do believe that the rational expectations/efficient markets theorem is a reasonable representation of financial markets, and a number of other large markets for homogeneous commodities, I do not believe that the labour market, or the markets for heterogeneous goods, can be described as efficient in this sense. Instead, I believe that market imperfections are pervasive in labour and goods markets, that capital markets are incomplete, that prices adjust relatively slowly, and that phenomena such as rationing, queuing and unemployment of resources occur all too frequently.

The model and the real world

I believe that Batchelor would agree that the model he actually sets out in his formal equations does indeed represent an *extreme* form of the rational expectations/efficient markets hypothesis. Thus, for example, equation 2 (in Box 1, page 61), states that the economy will *always* be at its full employment equilibrium, unless diverted from that equilibrium by a surprise shock. Since surprises, by definition, cannot be related to previous events, this would imply that variations of unemployment around its equilibrium level were also unrelated to previous events, and so would also imply that the state of the economy last year, last quarter, perhaps even yesterday, would have no implications whatsoever for the divergence, if any, from equilibrium of the economy today. It is clear, however, that there *is* persistence in the economy, and that equation 2 is simply not an adequate representation of the real world. I believe Batchelor would accept that, and I know that there are a number of developments by monetarist theorists which allow for persistence within the context of a broadly monetarist model.

The main question then at issue becomes one of whether *expected* monetary growth would, or would not, affect the current rate of growth of output. The argument of the monetarists is that it is only unanticipated monetary growth that has a real effect. While you can always surprise the economy, by a once-off unanticipated dose of monetary expansion, the short-term advantages of so doing, so it is argued, are more than offset by the longer-term effects both on inflation and, as he states, on uncertainty about future policy. So, the argument for monetary rules does not necessarily depend on the extreme form of the rational expectations/efficient markets theory which he sets down here.

Even though I accept that it is possible to set out the monetarist viewpoint in a more plausible, because less extreme, form, I still doubt whether the crucial feature of such a revised model, which is that expected monetary growth would have no effect on the real economy, can be supported. I doubt this for a number of reasons. I do not believe that the broad range of econometric results, for example those of Mishkin,[1] give much support to the hypothesis. Furthermore, I very much doubt whether either announcements, or expectations, or future short-term monetary growth have much effect on wage bargaining. Let us try a thought experiment. Assume that the Chancellor of the Exchequer at the next budget states that the rate of growth of M0 that he is aiming for will be 5 per cent higher than he had previously announced as his target for that year. What would you reckon would be the immediate impact on wage negotiations? Do you believe that wage negotiators would immediately settle for 5 per cent more? If not, is that because in your view his announcement would lack credibility? Or, do you believe that uncertainty about the true model of the economy, about likely velocity, and a host of other institutional reasons, break the simple links that the monetarists assume between monetary announcements and their effects on wages and prices?

Optimal control methods

Next, I want to turn to the issue of optimal control, which Batchelor touches on from time to time. What worries me about his approach is that there is insufficient realisation of the importance of the *time-horizon* in assessing the issue of the optimal method of control. Ever since the initial contribution of Bill Poole,[2] we have known that the issue of what to control is strongly influenced by the relative variability of the real economy, or the IS curve, as compared with the relative variability of financial markets, that is, the LM curve. But the relative variability of the real economy and the financial system respectively do not necessarily remain the same over all time-horizons. In the longer run, say, over a period of a year or more, the real economy is clearly capable of considerable variation while, under normal circumstances, the demand for money and other financial characteristics are reasonably stable and predictable. Thus, in the longer run, it does make more sense to try to control the rate of growth of monetary aggregates, allowing

[1] F. S. Mishkin, 'Does Anticipated Monetary Policy Matter? An Econometric Investigation', *Journal of Political Economy*, Vol. 90, 1982.
[2] W. Poole, 'Optimal Choice of Monetary Policy Instruments in a Single Stochastic Macro Model', *Quarterly Journal of Economics*, Vol. 84, No. 2, May 1970.

interest rates to vary up and down in line with the fluctuations in the IS curve.

The situation is not the same in the very short run. We all know how extremely variable financial markets can be in the very short run, and also how the demand for loans can vary, up and down, quite sharply depending on ephemeral circumstances, such as, for example, the date of application for British Gas shares. On the other hand, in the short run, from day-to-day or month-to-month, the real economy undoubtedly exhibits considerable inertia and stability. Thus, the shorter the time-horizon, the more the relative ranking of the variability in the real economy and the financial system tends to get reversed. Under these circumstances, what is clearly then desirable is to place more weight on stabilising interest rates in the very short run, and increasingly more weight on stabilising monetary growth in the longer run. This is essentially the operating policy which the authorities have, over the last 15 years or so, been following. I believe that Batchelor misses this, largely because he treats his optimal control theory in a timeless context, whereas the question of how one should seek to steer the economy does, in my view, depend quite crucially on the horizon within which you have to operate.

I know what Batchelor's response would be. He would argue that the medium- and longer-term considerations should be paramount, and that the achievement of longer-term control would be weakened by seeking to operate on interest rates in the short run. Indeed, I can conceive of some models of the working of the financial system in which that would be true. In the world in which we actually live, however, and particularly a world in which borrowers and savers react to interest-rate changes with some considerable lag, I do not believe that in practice one does weaken the ability to hit medium- and longer-term targets by the shorter-term operation of an interest-rate policy. Indeed, I believe the reverse: that any attempt to operate a system of monetary base control on a short-run day-to-day basis would be so disruptive in practice as to damage the longer-term control objectives.

Should Britain Join the EMS?

Let me turn next to Batchelor's analysis of whether or not to join the EMS. As you know, I also am sceptical of the advantages, and likely success, of that policy, but my reasons for scepticism are very different from those that he puts forward, and I do not subscribe to his. I find his claim that 'the success of the MTFS has made the external discipline argument redundant' breath-taking in its optimism. Moreover, I believe that his main supporting claim that 'There are well-developed forward markets in which exchange-rate risk can be hedged' is, unfortunately, simply not accurate over the time-horizons that would be appropriate. Well-developed forward markets really extend only for about six months, and at most up to about a year. Since capital equipment and buildings last for very much longer, it is simply not possible to hedge the risk of finding one's investment becoming unprofitable as a result of misalignment. Moreover, even if one could sell one's output in forward markets, in order to be fully hedged, it would also be necessary to be able to buy all one's inputs forward also. The claim that forward markets are sufficiently advanced to provide businessmen with sufficient protection against the kind of longer-term misalignment which has occurred in the UK and the USA is, unfortunately, simply wrong.

Role for indices of monetary growth

I am happy to turn next to a section of Batchelor's paper to which I can give more support—his advocacy of paying more attention to Divisia-type indices[3] of monetary growth. In a period when one of the major innovations represents the payment of more market-related interest rates on monetary aggregates, which undoubtedly is having considerable effect on the attractions of holding such deposits, it does seem to me to be worthwhile to construct and present such weighted monetary aggregates. I might, perhaps, add that Terry Mills, who did a great deal of work with me while at the Bank of England in assessing the relationship between monetary growth and nominal incomes, also wrote a paper analysing the application of such Divisia indices to monetary growth in the UK. This paper is to be found in the Bank of England technical paper series.[4]

---

[3] By this is meant indices which weight a variety of many measures into one, according to the probability of their use in transactions.

[4] T. C. Mills, 'Composite monetary indicators for the United Kingdom; construction and empirical analysis', Bank of England Discussion Papers, Technical Series, No. 3, 1983.

Nevertheless, Batchelor is keen to have a monetary target which can affect general expectations. Whatever you may have felt about my thought-experiment of the impact of the Chancellor's announcement about an existing monetary aggregate on subsequent wage negotiations, how far do you believe that the ordinary employee, or even employer, would in current circumstances understand, or be much influenced by, such a complicated monetary construct? Even so, it *would* still be worth preparing and publishing such an index, since if it is, as I suspect, going to be the most stable indicator of monetary developments, in time people would probably be prepared to watch and use the index, in the same way that they currently use the retail price index, without worrying excessively about the technicalities of how it is put together.

Conclusion

Essentially, I believe that Batchelor is excessively optimistic. Thus, in his philosophy, equilibrium would be achieved and markets would clear perfectly, if only government would stop intervening in a muddle-headed way and foul things up. Equally, the collapse in the stability of the relationship between £M3 and nominal incomes can be patched up by going to some better monetary aggregate. I rather doubt the latter. The pace of innovation, the increasing fuzziness about the definition of money itself, the fact that such monetary stability has been found wanting in a range of other countries which have also dropped monetary targets—all this makes me feel that for the foreseeable future—by which I mean in this respect the next four years—I doubt very much whether we can rely at all heavily on monetary targets as a financial anchor. I doubt whether we can rely instead on entry into a pegged exchange rate mechanism such as the EMS. If so, I cannot see any credible financial anchor to which the authorities can attach themselves. But, on the other hand, I am persuaded of the importance of having some financial anchor, in order to provide some backbone to discretionary policy, and to prevent a myopic preference for more demand expansion leading the UK once again back into stagflation. So, whereas Batchelor is an optimist, I am becoming increasingly pessimistic. I see the argument for rules, but I see no really credible rule which the authorities can, in the present political climate, adopt at this time.

Commentary—2
HAROLD ROSE
Economic Advisor, Barclays Bank

Roy Batchelor's paper makes three main points, apart from questions of terminology.

The first is the contention that the MTFS involved an unnecessary loss of output owing to the insufficient credibility of monetary policy and that this was due not only to the breakdown of £M3 as an inflation predictor but also to the proliferation of monetary indicators. But the addition of indicators to £M3 dates mainly from 1982, whereas the main loss in output took place in 1980, the result of a lack of credibility of the 1979 change in policy régime itself and emanating from events before the introduction of the MTFS. This raises issues outside the subject of his paper.

Even if inflation has been less than expected over the past few years, it does not necessarily follow that output has been adversely affected. The extent of the fall in inflation since 1983 has owed much to the drop in the prices of imported commodities. It is hard to see why output should be depressed by unexpected losses on stock values if the drop in imported input costs raises cash flows and *ex ante* profit margins. This kind of factor may be covered by the disturbance term in the (deliberately simple) model Batchelor uses; but, even so, his conclusion does not necessarily follow.

The 'counterparts' thesis

Batchelor's second thesis is that, because of the unreliability of successive monetary aggregates as inflation predictors, the choice of target should be made on *a priori* grounds. He shows that the 'counterparts' version of £M3, consisting of an accounting identity, can be made to apply to *any* definition of money stock, and that one feature of £M3 is that it contains a bank lending counterpart. Batchelor concludes that the emphasis placed on £M3 was only the echo of the long-standing preoccupation of British policy with 'credit' rather than with 'money'.

However, whatever its other faults, the fact that £M3 has a bank lending counterpart helps to distinguish between changes in demand and supply. If we observe a large change in bank lending, we are pretty safe in assuming that a change in the *supply* of broad money is taking place, whatever is happening to the demand function. (The question of whether the acceleration of £M3 will prove excessive has been discussed too often to justify any further comment by me.)

Batchelor contends that the *a priori* grounds on which the choice of monetary target should be made are those of the 'transactions' use of the aggregate, which points to some narrow measure. Partly because the interest-bearing element in M1 is rising, his preference is for the monetary base.

Is M0 a credible inflation predictor?

M0 is a useful indicator of current money expenditure, and it has apparently been the most successful predictor of inflation since 1980 (but not always before then). I have several reservations, none of them new. The first is that it is very doubtful whether M0, at present at least, is a widely *credible* predictor of inflation. On *a priori* grounds, it is unlikely that the behaviour of notes and coin, in which the transaction cost of switching between deposits and currency is small, especially in a world of ATM networks, is in itself part of the inflation mechanism. The relatively steady velocity of M0 (around its upward trend) is not surprising in view of the fact that it is entirely demand-determined.

The demand for M0 (relative to deposits) does respond to interest rates; but the important question is whether its behaviour really gives any more information about the future, either to the Government or to the public, than the change in interest rates required to influence it. If, however, M0 is a proxy for current money income *and* wage setting reacts directly to interest-rate changes, I agree that the behaviour of M0 is a valuable guide to changes in interest rates within a monetarist framework.

Choice of monetary operating target

Batchelor's third thesis is that the choice of monetary operating target should be based primarily on the consequent uncertainty of the prices associated with it. He argues against joining the EMS on the grounds that uncertainty about exchange rates can be more effectively hedged against than can uncertainty about interest rates.

This seems to me to underestimate the extent of protection available against interest rate uncertainty, ranging from variable-rate borrowing, which protects lenders and borrowers against one 'real' effect of inflation uncertainty, to swaps and futures.

In spite of his concern with interest rate uncertainty in the exchange rate debate, Batchelor seems to favour targeting bank cash reserves. He argues that the threat that the Bank of England might not meet daily cash shortages would mean merely that the clearing banks would hold higher cash reserves. But if complete disruption were to be avoided, especially with an overdraft system, this would almost certainly require the banks to hold such large and variable excess cash reserves that the money multiplier would be even more uncertain than the demand-for-money function. Moreover, the cost of holding large non-interest-bearing cash reserves would tend to divert lending to non-bank channels—as did the 'corset'.

I agree that the MTFS has been a valuable commitment to lowering inflation, despite all its difficulties. It is hard to see what equivalent commitment could have been designed in terms of interest rate policy alone, as Batchelor demonstrates. As far as the output loss is concerned, it is often overlooked that the increase in GDP between 1979 and 1985 was no different from that between 1973 and 1979. The larger rise in unemployment since 1979, therefore, has been due to a change in the relationship between output and employment; and this needs a different kind of explanation, such as that put forward by Beenstock and Minford in their paper.

The problem of monetary policy today, unless targeting M0 is sufficient, is obviously that of interpreting the behaviour of interest-bearing deposits as well as that of controlling it.

These difficulties have led the Chancellor towards an emphasis on fiscal and exchange rate policy intentions. The main weakness of the policy at present, apart from what I see as a lack of consistency between the two, or perhaps because of it, is its inadequate credibility. Mainly for that reason I would support full entry into the EMS, even though that, too, will undoubtedly present difficulties. But credibility is at least half the anti-inflation battle.

3. Innovative Supply-side Policies to Reduce Unemployment

RICHARD JACKMAN and RICHARD LAYARD
Centre for Labour Economics, London School of Economics and Political Science

With Commentaries by

D. A. PEEL
University College of Wales, Aberystwyth

and

SAMUEL BRITTAN
Financial Times

The Authors

RICHARD JACKMAN was born in 1945 and educated at St. Paul's School and Churchill College, Cambridge, where he graduated in 1967. He has recently been appointed Reader in Economics at the London School of Economics, where he has been Lecturer and Senior Lecturer since 1968.

His publications include *Economics of Inflation*; 'Keynes and Leijonhufvud' (*Oxford Economic Papers*, July 1974); 'University Efficiency and University Finance' (with Richard Layard, published in *Essays in Modern Economics*, ed. Michael Parkin, 1973); 'The Problem of Externalities in a Spatial Economy' (in *Regional Science—New Concepts and Old Problems*, ed. E. L. Cripps, 1975); *A Job Guarantee for Long-Term Unemployed People* (Employment Institute, 1986); and several collaborations with Richard Layard.

P. R. G. (RICHARD) LAYARD was born in 1934 and educated at King's College, Cambridge (where he was a Major Scholar), 1954-57. He has been Professor of Economics at the London School of Economics since 1980. He is also Head of the Centre for Labour Economics there. After reading History at Cambridge (First Class Honours), he taught in a comprehensive school for two years and then became senior research officer for the Robbins Committee on Higher Education, 1961-63. In 1964 he joined the LSE as Deputy Director of the Higher Education Research Unit, and converted to Economics by taking the M.Sc. part time with a Distinction. He joined the Economics Department as a Lecturer in 1968, becoming Reader in the Economics of Labour in 1975. Professor Layard is Chairman of the Employment Institute, and a Member of the University Grants Committee.

Professor Layard's books, mostly co-authored, include *Microeconomic Theory* (1978), and *The Causes of Poverty* (a Background Paper for the Royal Commission on the Distribution of Income and Wealth, 1978). He edited *Cost-Benefit Analysis* (1973). His Inaugural Lecture at the LSE, 'Is Incomes Policy the Answer to Unemployment?', was published in *Economica* (August 1982). The most recent of his many published books are *How to Beat Unemployment* (1986); *Economica Unemployment Supplement* (with C. Bean and S. Nickell, 1986); *Handbook of Labor Economics* (ed. with O. Ashenfelter, 1987); and *The Performance of the British Economy* (ed. with R. Dornbusch, forthcoming).

INTRODUCTION

The main constraint on non-inflationary growth in Britain comes from the labour market.[1] Policies to reduce the natural rate of unemployment must therefore lie at the heart of supply-side economics. In this paper we consider three sets of policies to reduce the natural rate:

   (i) policies to reduce the duration of long-term unemployment;
  (ii) tax-based incomes policies;
 (iii) shorter working hours and early retirement.

We strongly recommend the first two, and oppose the third.

The problem of inflation arises as follows. Wage-setters set wages as a mark-up on expected prices, and price-setters set prices as a mark-up on expected wages. If the mark-ups are too high, total claims exceed the size of the total cake available. The only possible upshot is rising inflation, as wages and prices leap-frog each other. The natural rate is where the two intended mark-ups are compatible with each other. Unemployment is the mechanism which brings about the compatibility.

This mechanism is illustrated in Figure 1. The intended real wage underlying wage-setting is reduced by high unemployment. This effect brings the 'target' real wage of wage-setters into line with the 'feasible' real wage based on price-setting.[2]

This analysis makes it clear that the aim of policy is to reduce wage-pressure in the wage-setting equation. There are three key propositions that we wish to exploit.

1. The long-term unemployed have no effect on wage pressure (evidence below, pp. 96-98). Thus measures to reduce long-term unemployment reduce the natural rate. In terms of Figure 1 they shift the wage-setting equation to the left.

2. Wage-setters are influenced by the cost of increasing wages. The aim should therefore be to increase the cost of wage increases to firms. This move will discourage firms from raising wages, and will also face unions with the prospect of higher job-loss from

---

[1] Long-run problems of competitiveness also stem mainly from the labour market. We also believe that capital generally adapts if higher demand is clearly expected (Modigliani *et al.* [1986]).

[2] For simplicity we have drawn the feasible wage independent of employment, so that real wages are never too high or too low. The problem is real-wage pressure, not actual real wages. We discuss the issue further below, p. 105.

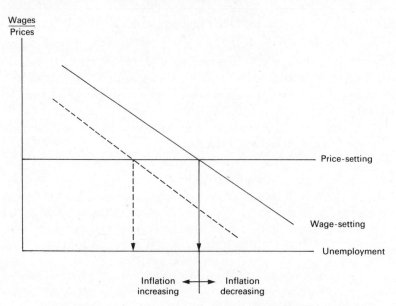

Figure 1: Real Wages, Unemployment and Inflation

any excess wage increases. This threat will also shift the wage-setting equation to the left.

3. There is no evidence that shorter working hours or early retirement have this effect. They thus make no contribution to the objectives of decreasing unemployment, and at the same time they decrease output—hardly the way to improve the supply side!

I. A JOB GUARANTEE FOR THE LONG-TERM UNEMPLOYED[3]

Evidence

Three independent pieces of evidence suggest strongly that long-term unemployment does much less to reduce wage pressure than short-term unemployment. The first is the work of Layard and Nickell [1986a] which suggests that wage pressure falls with total unemployment but is higher the larger the fraction of long-term

---

[3] This section draws heavily on Jackman *et al.* [1986].

unemployed within that total. At the current volume of long-term unemployment, reductions in it would not increase wage pressure at all.[4]

A second study suggests a mechanism which might account for the findings of the first. As is well known, the volume of unemployment at a given rate of vacancies has risen over time. Budd, Levine and Smith [1986] show that this increase is partly due to the rise in long-term unemployment (as a fraction of total unemployment)—an assessment consistent with the view that the long-term unemployed are less effective members of the labour market than the short-term unemployed.[5]

Third, the proportion of the long-term unemployed who leave unemployment is much less than for the short-term unemployed.

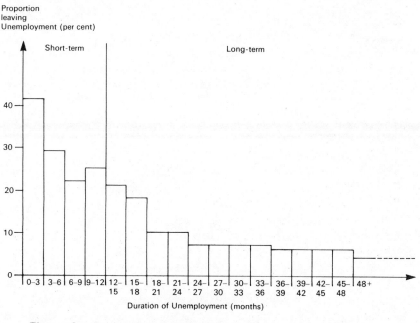

Figure 2: Proportion Leaving Unemployment in a Quarter by Duration
(First quarter 1984)

Source: Jackman *et al.* [1986].

---

[4] Layard and Nickell [1986a], equation 7.
[5] Appendix 1, p. 115.

Someone unemployed for over four years is *10 times* less likely to leave unemployment in the next quarter than someone recently made unemployed (Figure 2).[6] This discrepancy is partly because the long-term unemployed become demoralised and seek work less effectively than the short-term unemployed, and partly because employers are less keen to hire them (Jackman *et al.* [1986], Tables 2.3 and 2.4). In consequence, they have been effectively detached from the labour force. It is, as Gavyn Davies has said, as if they had been sent to Australia.

A major objective of policy should therefore be to re-integrate them and re-establish their connections with employers and the world of work.

A job guarantee

In order to establish this objective as a top priority, we propose that within three years the government should be in a position to guarantee an offer of a one-year job to all the long-term unemployed.[7] There are now 1.35 million long-term unemployed and, for reasons given below, the job guarantee would be achieved by means of one million government-supported places each year. These might be provided through the MSC as follows:

   (i) 250,000 places on the Community Programme.

   (ii) 200,000 places on a major new Building Improvement Programme. Local authorities, hospitals and deserving private agents could propose projects. The MSC would choose among the projects (one criterion being that it would not otherwise have taken place) and then put them out to tender from private contractors. Successful private contractors would be expected to employ a high proportion of long-term unemployed people on the projects, paid at the market rate for the job for a full week's work. The subsidised employment would be explicitly for one year, but one would hope that many of the workers could continue thereafter with the same employer.

---

[6] The pattern in Figure 2 *cannot* be explained mainly by the fact that people who are likely to find a job continue disproportionately into long-term unemployment (Jackman and Layard [1986]).

[7] Layard, Metcalf and O'Brien [1986], Employment Committee [1986a and 1986b], and Jackman *et al.* [1986b].

(iii) 50,000 places for long-term unemployed people in social services and health, paid the rate for the job. These would again be one-year jobs, but one would hope that, because of turnover, many of the individuals could be retained thereafter.

(iv) 100,000 places on training schemes, paid at benefit plus £20 a week.

(v) 400,000 places in the rest of the economy, where employers would be paid £2,000 for a year for each long-term unemployed person they employed for that period. Again, one would hope that, because of turnover, many of the individuals would stay on with the same employer thereafter.

Analysis

We must now discuss the likely effects of the scheme and the rationale for its design. We shall assume that the long-term unemployed have no effect on wage pressure. This assumption implies that the natural rate of unemployment must be defined entirely in relation to short-term unemployment. Since wage infla-tion has been constant for the last four years, we shall assume that the British economy is now at the natural rate of short-term unemployment.[8] (Note that this assumption eliminates the scope for 'multiplier' effects on demand.) For the discussion in this section we therefore take short-term unemployment as given, which means that the inflow into *long-term* unemployment is also given. *The object of policy is then to reduce the duration of long-term unemployment* (Figure 3).

Unless there is compulsion to accept the job guarantee the moment you become unemployed for over a year, long-term unemployment cannot be completely eliminated. But we can con-siderably accelerate the outflow rate, making it more like the outflow rate from short-term unemployment. At present 40 per cent of the short-term unemployed leave within a quarter.[9] If we

---

[8] In Section II we shall discuss how to change this by tax-based incomes policy.

[9] That is, the ratio of outflow to stock. The outflow includes those who flow out within a quarter. By contrast Figure 2 includes under a half of those who flow out within the first three months. (It relates to the subsequent history of those who were unemployed at a particular date in January and does not include those who became unemployed between January and March and then found work in the same quarter.)

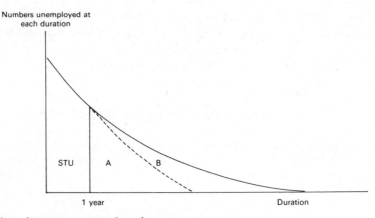

Numbers unemployed at each duration

STU   A   B

1 year   Duration

STU   = short-term unemployed
A+B   = long-term unemployed: no job guarantee
A   = long-term unemployed: job guarantee

Figure 3: Effects of Policy on the Long-term Unemployed

could achieve the same for the long-term unemployed, the average duration of long-term unemployment would become $2\frac{1}{2}$ quarters (i.e. 100/40). With an inflow of one million a year into long-term unemployment, the stock of long-term unemployed would become roughly 0.6 million—rather less than half of what it is now.[10]

So how would the extra jobs have been created? The experience of work (or training) raises the effective supply of labour. Since the labour market adjusts to this increased supply, more jobs will be created.

This effect is illustrated in Figure 4. Short-term unemployment is constant. Long-term unemployment falls. Some of the extra jobs are the 350,000 places on the Building Improvement Programme, Social Services and Health and Training Programmes, but there are an additional 400,000 places with other employers.[11]

---

[10] The outflow rate into employment outside construction, social services and health would have risen only from 0.35/1.35 to 0.4/0.6.

[11] That this equals the annual flow into subsidised employment is simply a chance outcome of our numerical assumption about the duration of long-term unemployment.

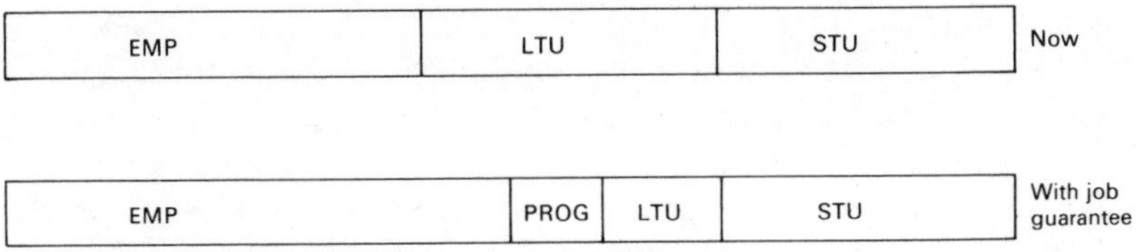

EMP		LTU	STU	Now

EMP		PROG	LTU	STU	With job guarantee

EMP = employment
LTU = long-term unemployment
STU = short-term unemployment
PROG = Building Improvement Programme, Social Services and Health and Training, but *not* subsidised recruitment scheme.

Figure 4: Division of the Labour Force into Different Activities

It is natural to ask about the dynamics through which these results would come about. As the effective supply of labour grows, short-term unemployment tends to rise (in part because people off the scheme fail to find jobs). This rise then sets in motion the normal supply-side forces which tend to increase employment. (The process would, of course, be eased if demand were deliberately increased at this stage.)

Cost

We turn now to the cost-effectiveness of our proposals. In evaluating special measures the normal procedure is to ask, first, how the number of places subsidised compares with the number of net jobs created. The normal arithmetic is as follows:

Net jobs created = Jobs paid for *minus* Substitution *minus* Displacement *minus* Deadweight.

'Substitution' and 'displacement' refer to other jobs destroyed, and 'deadweight' to jobs paid for which would have existed anyway. In our framework these three concepts are unhelpful.

Displacement and substitution

In our context, when long-term unemployed people are put into jobs which would otherwise have been done by others, short-term unemployment rises temporarily, but then reverts to its original level by the adjustment process just described. Thus in the medium term *there is no substitution nor displacement*. The remarkable thing about the current debate is that those who oppose special measures generally emphasise substitution and displacement effects, although these can exist only if there is a shortage of demand, which the same people generally deny to be the case.[12] Employment Ministers regularly express fears about displacement and substitution, asserting in the next breath that there is no shortage of demand.

By the same token, advocates of special measures should not be talking in terms of demand-side multiplier effects* (if the economy is now at the natural rate of short-term unemployment). If there are multipliers, they are on the supply side. It would be logically possible for the number of net new jobs to be either larger or smaller than the number of places subsidised. Given our particular numerical assumption about duration, the numbers are in fact equal (Table 1).

TABLE 1
STOCKS AND FLOWS OF LONG-TERM UNEMPLOYED
(millions)

			Now	With Job guarantee
Stock			1.35	0.60
Inflow			1.00	1.00
Outflow	A	Community Programme	0.25	0.25
	B	Building Improvement Programme, Social Services and Health, Training	—	0.35
	C	Other employers	0.75	0.40
		Total	1.00	1.00

---

[12] *Cf.*, for example, *The Government's Reply to the Select Committee on Employment* [1986], and the White Paper on *Employment, the Challenge for the Nation*, Cmnd. 9474, HMSO, 1985, p. 12.

* That is, expansionary effects on employment over and above the direct expansionary effects of the measures.—ED.

Deadweight

The concept of deadweight is likewise unhelpful. In the steady state the numbers flowing out of long-term unemployment are bound to be the same with or without a job guarantee. But this does not mean there is 100 per cent deadweight, since they flow out quicker.

So what are the estimated costs? The gross costs once the scheme has built up are shown in Table 2.[13] To obtain the net cost we subtract the very substantial savings on unemployment benefits (£2.25 billion) and tax flow-back (£0.65 billion), amounting in all to nearly £3 billion—a net cost per job of less than £2,000 a year. The

TABLE 2

JOB GUARANTEE PROGRAMMES—A SUMMARY OF COSTINGS

Programme	Annual intake (thousands)	Gross cost per job (£ p.a.)	Total gross cost (£ bn. p.a.)
Building Improvement Programme	200	12,000	2.4
Recruitment Scheme	400	2,000	0.8
Training Scheme	100	6,000	0.6
Public Sector Scheme	50	8,000	0.4
	750		4.2

Public expenditure savings
Unemployment falls by 750,000 people at an average saving of £3,000 per year per person. — £2.25 bn.

Tax flowbacks
Employment increases by 650,000 people at an average wage of, say, £100 a week, leading to payment of national insurance and income tax of an average £1,000 per year per person — £0.65 bn.
Overall net cost of programme — £1.3 bn.
Overall net cost per job — £1,700

---

[13] Layard, Metcalf and O'Brien and the Employment Committee exaggerated the cost per place on the recruitment scheme by assuming that there was an additional 'deadweight' outflow of 500,000 people being hired into the private sector. Our present framework makes it clear that in the steady state such people would not exist. For a discussion of costs during the build-up of the scheme, Jackman *et al.*, Table 6.5 and related text.

gross cost is similar to that estimated by the Employment Committee but the savings are much higher and more accurately estimated.[14] There is therefore every reason to suppose that the Employment Committee estimate of £4,500 net cost per annum per job was an over-estimate, and the Government's estimate of £8,000- £9,000 (based on substitution and displacement) even more so. Even so, we would consider that on the Government's own costings the scheme is a best buy, and the most cost-effective way of using money to improve the supply side of the economy.

II. TAX-BASED INCOMES POLICY

As we have said, the central strategy for improving the supply side of the economy is to reduce pressure on wages. An obvious approach is to tackle the problem head on. While traditional incomes policies have had temporary successes (especially in the later 1970s), they have not generally been able to last very long. This failure occurs because they set an absolute limit on wage growth for individual grades of employee, which eliminates free collective bargaining (making it unacceptable to the unions) and severely reduces the scope for employers to raise wages, to recruit, retain and motivate workers (except by 'fiddles' like regrading). The obvious solution is to have a fixed norm for the growth of average earnings in each firm (without regard to grade structure), and to tax heavily any excess earnings growth—whilst not making it unlawful. This would exert a strong downwards pressure on excess wage growth, at the same time leaving much of the required flexibility intact.

We have discussed the pros *and* cons of this approach at length in other places.[15] Here we shall concentrate only on two issues of feasibility.

(1) To achieve results, does incomes policy have to reduce real take-home pay—making it likely that politicians will be unwilling to face the chorus of complaint?

(2) Can the Inland Revenue implement it effectively?

---

[14] The earlier work allowed only £40 a week in benefit compared with the now accurate figure of £60. It ignored taxes.

[15] Initially Layard [1982], Jackman and Layard [1982a and b], and, in a more popular form, Layard and Nickell [1986b].

Real wages and employment

In our earlier work we argued that the demand for labour in the economy as a whole would require a fall in the wage relative to product prices if there were to be an increase in employment. This proposition was an integral part of our approach. Our current theory is different and shows that even if the real product wage is independent of employment (as in Figure 1), tax-based incomes policy will work.

In Jackman and Layard [1986a] we assume that the marginal productivity of labour in volume terms is constant but that firms are monopolistic competitors in the product market. Workers therefore face a downwards-sloping demand for their labour, viewed as a function of the firm's wage relative to the general price level. If unions set wages, they will then be less inclined to push their luck if a rise of £1 in the wage raises the employer's labour cost by £$(1 + t)$ where t is the inflation-tax rate. In this context the effect of this restraint on their wage demands is to reduce the equilibrium unemployment rate to $1/(\eta - 1)(1 + t)$, a formula in which η is the elasticity of product demand with respect to its relative price. Thus falls in real wages are not necessarily part of the mechanism for achieving increases in employment by wage restraint. It would work even in a world in which prices were a constant mark-up on wage cost.

Whether the world is really like that is an empirical question. According to Layard and Nickell ([1986a], equation 1'), the mark-up of prices over wages increases by $\frac{1}{4}$ per cent for each percentage point fall in unemployment. Thus a 1 per cent fall in unemployment would reduce wages relative to the GDP deflator by $\frac{1}{4}$ per cent. To that extent the price-setting line in Figure 1 should slope upwards slightly.

There are three further points. First, increased economic activity raises the tax-base. If government expenditure is constant, a 1 per cent fall in unemployment makes it possible to cut tax rates by at least 1 percentage point. So after-tax real wages would rise by nearly $\frac{1}{2}$ per cent.[16] Secondly, the capital stock will rise, which will

---

[16] Constant balance requires $G = Yt + \text{constant}$,

$$\therefore \ d \log t = -d \log Y$$

$\therefore \ d \log [W(1 - t)] = d \log W - [t/(1 - t)] d \log t = -(\frac{1}{4} + \frac{2}{3})$ per cent (where $G = $ government expenditure, $t = $ average tax rate, $Y = $ national income, $W = $ wages per head).

further raise the feasible real wage. But, thirdly, a real depreciation will be required to balance the current account. Suppose that a 1 per cent fall in unemployment raises imports by $\frac{1}{2}$ per cent of GNP. If the sum of import and export price elasticities were 2 (implying a 2 per cent response of total trade volumes to a 1 per cent change in competitiveness), this would in Britain require a 2 per cent depreciation in real terms, or a $\frac{2}{3}$ per cent fall in the real wage relative to the retail price index (RPI) (rather than, as so far, to the GDP deflator). This fall almost exactly offsets our previous considerations, leaving living standards unaffected.

Not an administrative nightmare

Tax-based incomes policy would not, as is sometimes alleged, be an administrative nightmare.

The tax could be collected simply, at the same time as PAYE. The definition of earnings would be the same as for PAYE, so the Inland Revenue already have the basic details of the tax base. The firm would simply compute its average hourly earnings (averaged over all its employees), compare the result with the reference level, and send in a cheque to the Revenue. This would be done quarterly, by comparing earnings with those in the same quarter one year earlier. There would be no scrutiny of individual settlements, nor of the pay of any particular individual. At present the audit of the whole of PAYE and NI figures submitted by firms requires under 500 inspectors. So there is no reason the audit of the counter-inflation tax should require more than 100 or so additional inspectors.

This calculation assumes that the tax would be confined to firms with over 100 workers. Fewer than 20,000 companies would therefore be involved, compared with nearly one million pay-points for PAYE, thus saving considerably on administrative costs both to the Revenue and to firms. Most of the firms affected have computerised payrolls. Moreover, in large firms cheating is less likely both because firms value their reputations, and because a manager who cheated would be less likely to gain personally from cheating by the firm. To stop firms trying to avoid tax by setting up new firms to employ their more skilled workers, the tax would have to apply to the 'group' as a whole (that is, to any company *and* its subsidiaries).[17] But it would in practice be computed at each 'PAYE pay-

---

[17] Defined, say, as any company in which it had a 75 per cent stake or more.

point'. Genuinely new enterprises would be excluded. There might be problems connected with changes in the ownership of existing enterprises; but these can be handled with a sensible interpretation of 'continuity' of operations.

There are doubtless many ways in which firms will try to evade the tax. But this is true of all taxes. People tend to assume that existing taxes are securely founded, whilst any new ones are insecure in the extreme. On examination, however, it seems that a counter-inflation tax could be quite straightforward. It would be much less of a bureaucratic nightmare than a prolonged old-style incomes policy, with a Relativities Board and all that. Without something of this kind there is no hope of getting back to the unemployment rates of the later 1970s.

III. SHORTER WORKING HOURS AND EARLY RETIREMENT

Many people believe that, to reduce unemployment, working hours should be cut and early retirement encouraged. What are the arguments for and against these ideas?

The case for shorter working hours

Suppose that a nation is going to produce a certain amount of output, and that, roughly speaking, there is a certain total number of hours of work to be done each week. If there are unemployed people who are desperate to work, it would be much better to reduce the hours worked by each worker and increase the number of workers. This would allocate a given amount of work more fairly among those who were willing to work. And it would reduce unemployment.

The 'lump-of-output' fallacy

There can be no doubt that, *so long as output is unaffected*, this argument is decisive. But the question is: Would output be unaffected? We cannot take that for granted: that is the 'lump-of-output' fallacy. In fact, output is a key variable in the situation. So what would happen to it?

The first step is to ask what might happen to inflation. The evidence (below, p. 116) suggests that *any* steps which reduced unemployment would raise inflationary pressure (excluding, of course, measures such as those discussed in Sections I and II). The relationship involved is illustrated in Figure 5 and shows that, whenever unemployment is lower, inflation rises more (or falls less) than it otherwise would. This would happen whether unemployment were reduced by a general reflation (with increased output) *or* because hours per worker had been cut (with output fixed).

So what will happen if shorter hours or early retirement are used to cut unemployment? Inflation will rise more than it otherwise would. Two responses are then possible.

Some politicians and analysts might be prepared to accept rising inflation as the price of reduced unemployment. But if this is the reaction, it would obviously have been better to cut unemployment

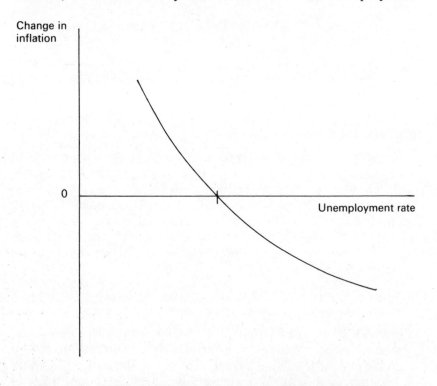

Figure 5: Effects of Unemployment on Changes in Inflation

by expanding output than by simply re-distributing a given amount of work over more people. So there is no case for shorter working hours along that route.

Along the alternative route the outlook is even bleaker. In this scenario the government sees inflation rising, decides that it is unacceptable, and allows unemployment to rise back to its original level (so as to control inflation). The net result of shorter working hours is then no reduction in unemployment, but a reduction in output.

Which response is the more likely? We cannot be sure. If shorter working hours have no effect on the trade-off between unemployment and inflation (shown in Figure 1), there is no obvious reason why they should affect the mix of unemployment and inflation that the government chooses.

But in any case the main effect of shorter working hours is clear. For *any* particular given rate of inflation, they lead to a lower volume of output, and make Britain a poorer nation.

Evidence on shorter working hours

The argument outlined so far depends crucially on the view that shorter hours do not reduce the inflationary pressure at any given level of unemployment. This conclusion is based on work by David Grubb summarised in Appendix 2 (below, p. 116). This showed clearly that for 19 OECD countries, working hours had no effect on the degree of inflationary pressure.

Going further, one could ask how working hours have affected unemployment itself. We have not attempted to examine this relationship directly (rather than indirectly through the effect on inflationary pressure). But it is interesting to see how changes in working hours and in unemployment in different countries compare. So Figure 6 shows for each of nine countries how working hours and unemployment have changed in the last 10 years. Average hours have fallen most in the UK, the Netherlands and France (about 8 per cent in each). They have barely fallen in the USA and have actually risen in Japan. And what about unemployment? Unemployment has risen most in those countries where working hours have fallen most. The case for shorter working hours receives no support from these figures.

Of course, one would certainly not argue from these figures that

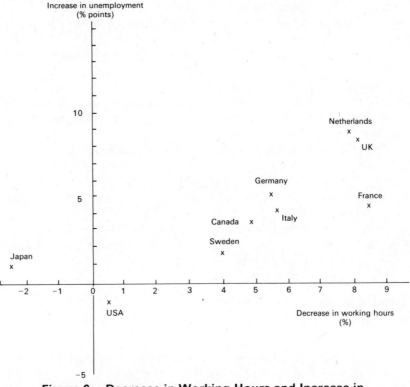

Figure 6: Decrease in Working Hours and Increase in Unemployment, 1975-85

Notes: 1. Average hours are average annual hours per person in employment.
2. Changes in Japan, Netherlands, Sweden, UK are for 1975–84, and in France for 1975–83.

Source: OECD *Employment Outlook*, September 1986, pp. 140 and 142.

shorter working hours have *caused* higher unemployment. For the comparison is not carried out with other variables held constant. And to some extent the forces which have raised unemployment in the UK, the Netherlands and France may have also reduced working hours. But there are two key points about Figure 6. First, it covers a 10-year period, which allows at least some abstraction from the short-term cyclical factors which would tend to produce the inverse correlation observed. Second, and more important, any gains in employment obtained from shorter working hours cannot have been large if the inverse correlation in the figures is so large.

110

Shorter working hours certainly seem to offer little protection against unemployment, and the burden of proof is now very firmly on those who favour them.

The case for early retirement

Does more early retirement offer a better hope? Again, the case for it is clear. *If* output is unaffected, it should be produced by those who most want work. If there are some people in work who would not mind retiring, while others out of work are desperate for a job, humanity requires that the older ones make way for those who really want the work.

The lump-of-output fallacy again

But, once again, why take output as given? How will it respond to more early retirement? This depends on how inflation would be affected if more people left the labour force. If output is unchanged, the numbers of jobs remain the same; so, when workers retire, unemployment falls.

According to Figure 1, inflation therefore rises more than it would otherwise. And this is what the evidence shows. In his work on 19 OECD countries (shown in Appendix 2), David Grubb asked if inflationary pressure rises as much when the labour force is reduced (thus cutting unemployment) as when employment increases (thus again cutting unemployment). The answer was that it does. The effect is exactly the same and nearly as well-defined.

So early retirement is not an easy option either. If the number of jobs remains constant, and some workers retire, inflation will increase.

Once again, there are two possible responses. One is to accept the extra inflation. But, again, it would surely have been better to generate the extra inflation by providing more jobs than by simply shuffling the existing jobs around. Alternatively, the government might choose a similar mix of inflation and unemployment to that which it would have chosen otherwise. Hence unemployment will revert to its former rate. But there will now be fewer jobs, because the labour force has shrunk. On either response the result, for a given inflation, will be fewer jobs and lower output. The nation will be poorer.

Evidence on early retirement

How do changes in early retirement in the last 10 years compare with changes in employment? This is shown in Figure 7. The horizontal axis shows the change in the percentage of men aged 55 to 64 in the labour force. Again, the increase in early retirement has been largest in the UK, the Netherlands and France. It has been lowest in Japan. Once again, the countries that have experienced more early retirement (often encouraged by government policy) are those with the biggest rise in unemployment. The causal mechanism

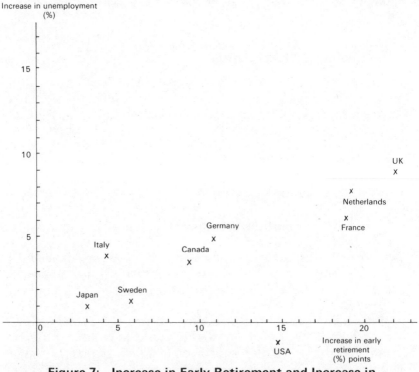

Figure 7: Increase in Early Retirement and Increase in Unemployment, 1975–85

(Increase in early retirement=Fall in percentage of males aged 55–64 in labour force)

Notes: Italy, 1975–84; men aged 60–64.
Sources: OECD *Labour Force Statistics*, 1964–84, Part III, pp. 468–497.
 OECD *Employment Outlook*, September 1986, p. 140.

is unclear; but the burden of proof is again surely on those who believe that more early retirement would help avoid unemployment.

Conclusion

To many people, shorter working hours and early retirement appear to be common-sense solutions for unemployment. But they are not, because they are not based on any theory of what determines unemployment. The only theory behind them is the lump-of-output theory—that output is a given. In this paper we have argued that output is not a given. If it were, shorter working hours would, of course, reduce unemployment. But that would increase inflationary pressure. Given any particular set of preferences, the government would be likely to choose the original rate of unemployment, and the only result would then be a fall in output. The same applies to early retirement. If output were constant, this *would* reduce unemployment. But that effect would in turn generate inflationary pressure, and might well lead to a deflation of output to contain inflation, with unemployment back to its former level.

If, on the other hand, we are willing to tolerate the risk of higher inflation, we should make sure we get higher output in return. Shorter working hours and early retirement cannot therefore be recommended, whatever assumption one makes about the tolerable rate of inflation.

All this is shown in Figure 8, but we hope the argument is clear by now. The conclusion is that this is not the way to deal with unemployment. It *may* be desirable on other grounds, as part of a very long-term change in patterns of life. As a country gets richer, its men (though not its women) tend to work fewer paid hours per week and fewer years per lifetime. This is admirable, but it is a consequence of affluence. And it is a trend which should not be confused with the completely different question of how policy should respond to economic misfortune. To respond to misfortune by making ourselves poorer is not common sense.

Instead, policy should seek to expand the use of national resources, not to reduce it. We have to create more full-time jobs in ways that do not increase inflation. By targeted reflation and sensible incomes policies the relationship between inflation and unemployment shown in Figure 5 can be shifted to the left. But this

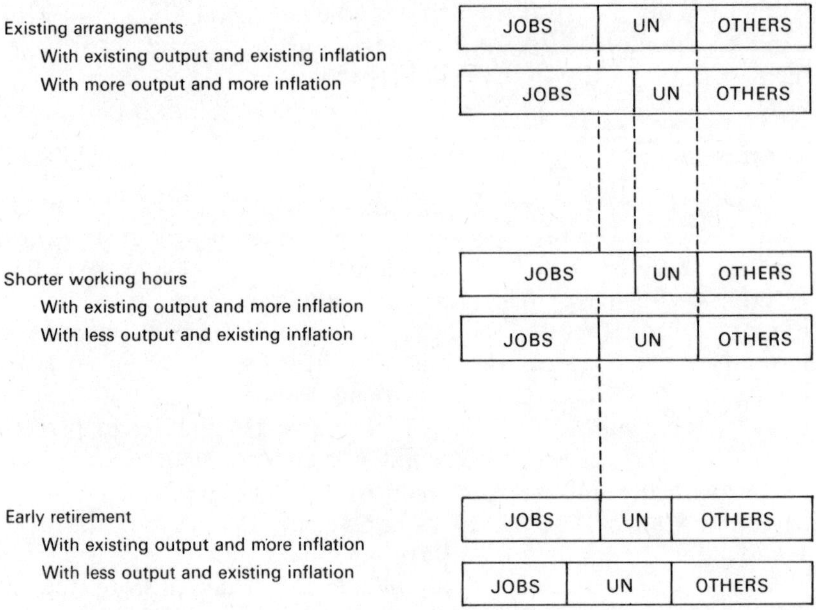

Existing arrangements			
JOBS	UN	OTHERS

With existing output and existing inflation
With more output and more inflation

JOBS	UN	OTHERS

Shorter working hours			
JOBS	UN	OTHERS

With existing output and more inflation
With less output and existing inflation

JOBS	UN	OTHERS

Early retirement			
JOBS	UN	OTHERS

With existing output and more inflation
With less output and existing inflation

JOBS	UN	OTHERS

Figure 8: Economic Activity

This diagram shows how the total population is divided between those in jobs, those unemployed, and those not in the labour force (including the retired).

result cannot be achieved either by shorter working hours or by early retirement. On these matters, we should do better to follow the bold example of the USA and Japan, and not the timid one of Europe.

APPENDIX 1

Interpretation of the shift of the u/v curve

Suppose a steady state where the exits from unemployment equal the entries (= sN where N is employment and s the separation rate into unemployment). Suppose also that the probability of a given individual leaving unemployment when he has been unemployed d periods is

$$c \ p(d) \ g \left(\frac{V}{cU \sum_d p(d) \, f(d)} \right)$$

where c is a common effect affecting the rate of matching workers to jobs, p(d) is the effect of duration ($p' < 0$), and g( ) is the effect of general economic opportunities (with $g' > 0$, g( ) less than unit elastic). U is the number unemployed and V the number of vacancies, and f(d) the proportion of unemployed with duration d. It follows that in the steady state

$$sN = Uc \ g \left(\frac{V}{cU \sum_d p(d) \, f(d)} \right) \sum_d p(d) \, f(d).$$

Hence

$$s = uc \ g \left(\frac{v}{cu \sum_d p(d) \, f(d)} \right) \sum_d p(d) \, f(d).$$

where $u = v/N$ and $v = V/N$. Hence

$$s = h[u, v, c, \sum_d p(d) \, f(d)].$$
$$+ \ + \ + \quad \ +$$

This gives the u/v curve. If for some reason durations lengthen with a constant, the last term falls and u rises for given v.[18] That the u/v curve shifted out when the proportion of long-term unemployed (R) rose is thus consistent with the theory that $p' < 0$.

There could, however, be an alternative explanation. Suppose $p' = 0$ and Figure 2 is entirely due to heterogeneity among those who become unemployed. Then *if* c fell, the u/v curve would shift out *and* R would rise. If we could not observe c we would be tempted to attribute the shift in the u/v curve to the rise in R. But there is no reason that there should in the last six years have been an exogenous fall in c—quite the contrary. For other evidence against the heterogeneity approach, Jackman and Layard [1986b].

---

[18] Of course, in the long run the distribution of d will be related to u and there will be a flatter u/v curve in which the last term has been substituted out.

APPENDIX 2

The effect of hours and of labour force upon wages

David Grubb has performed the following regressions (average co-efficients and t-statistics for 19 OECD countries from 1952 to 1982):

$$\dot{w} = \text{constant} + 0.70\dot{p}_{-1} + 0.30w_{-1} - 0.33(w-p)_{-1}$$

$$(3.0) \qquad (1.5)$$

$$- 1.91 + 2.0n - 0.2h + 0.2t,$$

$$(1.6) \quad (2.3) \quad (0.2) \quad (0.3)$$

where $w = \log$ hourly earnings in manufacturing, $p = \log$ prices (consumption deflator), $l = \log$ labour force, $n = \log$ employment, $h = \log$ average weekly hours per worker in manufacturing, and $t = \text{time}$. This shows that hours per worker play no role, and that a decrease in the labour force generates as much wage pressure as an equal increase in employment. For further details of this work, D. Grubb, 'Topics in the OECD Phillips Curve', *Economic Journal*, Vol. 96, No. 381, March 1986, pp. 55-80.

For a brief theoretical discussion of why hours of work might not affect unemployment, R. Layard, *How to Beat Unemployment*, Oxford University Press, 1986, pp. 179-180.

REFERENCES

Budd, A., Levine, P., and Smith, P. [1986]: 'Unemployment, Vacancies and the Long-Term Unemployed', Discussion Paper No. 154, Centre for Economic Forecasting, London Business School.

Employment Committee of the House of Commons [1986]: First Report 1985-86: *Special Employment Measures and the Long-Term Unemployed*, January.

Employment Committee of the House of Commons [1986]: Third Report 1985-86: *The Government's Reply to the Select Committee's Report on Special Measures and the Long-Term Unemployed*, June.

Jackman, R., and Layard, R. [1982a]: 'An Inflation Tax', *Fiscal Studies*, March.

Jackman, R., and Layard, R. [1982b]: 'Trade Unions, the NAIRU and a Wage-Inflation Tax', *Economica*, August.

Jackman, R., and Layard, R. [1986a]: 'A Wage-Tax, Worker-

Subsidy Policy for Reducing the "Natural" Rate of Unemployment', in W. Beckerman (ed.), *Wage Rigidity and Unemployment*, Duckworth.

Jackman, R., and Layard, R. [1986b]: 'Does Long-Term Unemployment Reduce a Person's Chance of A Job? A New Test', Working Paper No. 883, Centre for Labour Economics, London School of Economics.

Jackman, R., *et al.* [1986]: *A Job Guarantee for Long-Term Unemployed People*, Employment Institute, December.

Layard, R. [1982]: 'Is Incomes Policy the Answer to Unemployment?', *Economica*, August.

Layard, R., Metcalf, D., and O'Brien, R. [1986]: 'A New Deal for the Long-Term Unemployed', in P. E. Hart (ed.), *Unemployment and Labour Market Policies*, Gower.

Layard, R., and Nickell, S. [1986a]: 'The Performance of the British Labour Market', in R. Dornbusch and R. Layard (eds.), *The Performance of the British Economy*, Oxford University Press (forthcoming).

Layard, R., and Nickell, S. [1986b]: *An Incomes Policy to Help the Unemployed*, Employment Institute, November.

Modigliani, F., Monti, M., Dreze, J., Giersch, H., and Layard, R. [1986]: *Reducing Unemployment in Europe: The Role of Capital Formation*, CEPS Papers No. 28, Centre for European Policy Studies.

Commentary—1

D. A. PEEL
University College of Wales, Aberystwyth

I always look forward to reading papers by Professor Layard and Dr Jackman since I invariably find them stimulating, and ultimately, thought provoking. This has been no exception. So far the following points have occurred to me.

Jackman and Layard's policy prescriptions flow from their view on the working of the economic system. As far as I am aware, they have not as yet published a formal stylised macro-economic model which represents their views. On the basis of their paper today, and Professor Layard's book, *How to Beat Unemployment*, it would, I believe, embody some empirically questionable and possibly inconsistent features.

It is made clear in their analysis of the Phillips curve that inflation expectations are formed adaptively, that is, by projecting the past trends in inflation, rather than in an informed manner. This assumption leads them, I believe, not to make the appropriate theoretical distinction in their analysis between the transitional and permanent effects of their policy prescriptions on inflation. For example, when considering retirement or shorter working hours, which presumably occur by *diktat*, the first step in their analysis is to consider the implications for inflation, even though no monetary implications, *per se*, are implied by the *diktat*. Their analysis is based on empirical results derived from estimates of a Phillips curve, with hours, employment and labour force as explanatory variables. This, I believe, is inappropriate. The flow dimensions of labour services, demanded and supplied, must be integrated formally into the Phillips curve model, not appended in an *ad hoc* fashion.

A balanced-budget perspective

It would, I believe, have been more appropriate to consider this issue from the perspective of a balanced budget (as they often do with tax-based incomes policies (TIP)), when expectations of inflation are realised, and a formal model of the labour market, which explicitly recognises the flow dimension of labour services. From this perspective, changes in hours of work or retirement caused by effective *diktat* are likely in many models to increase real wage costs to employers, probably leading to reduced employment, and an increased level of measured unemployment; and they cause temporary changes in the rate of inflation. But, if hours of work are reduced because of a reduction in employment protection, or in taxes on employment or the abolition of investment incentives, then we are likely to predict an increase in the stock demand for labour and, *ceteris paribus*, a fall in the natural rate because these measures lower the relative cost of labour (on the books) as a factor of production. Indeed, I believe Professor Layard (and Steve Nickell) suggested recently that unemployment has been 3 per cent higher because of employment protection.[1]

Tax-based incomes policies

Turning next to their advocacy of TIP, I am now uncertain precisely what the authors are claiming for it. I used to believe, on the basis of their earlier formal models, that their advocacy of TIP was based on its potential to make the demand curve for labour more elastic, giving optimising unions the incentive to choose higher employment and lower real wages in equilibrium. TIP, in other words, is a policy devised to reduce the natural rate of unemployment, with essentially one-shot effects on the rate of wage or price inflation in equilibrium. If one could close one's eyes to the potential administrative costs and other distortions, in this form, TIP might find some support as a second-best measure, if direct measures to tackle union monopoly power are politically unacceptable. But Professor Layard, in his book, repeatedly claims that to control money wage inflation an incomes policy, namely TIP, is essential. He writes, for instance, about the 1978-79 period:

> 'in retrospect, it is clear that one could not possibly have had the almost tolerable level of unemployment at one and a quarter million had we not had the incomes policy. It is essential that once again we allow ourselves this weapon against *inflation*—but we do not have to keep the same kind of incomes policy';

---

[1] R. Layard and S. Nickell, 'Unemployment in Britain', *Economica*, Supplement, 1986.

and, when discussing aggregate demand policy:

> 'we should remember that prices depend essentially on wages and the price of imports. We have already taken enormous pains to avoid any extra wage inflation' (Layard [1986], p. 93 [namely TIP: my insertion]).

Since I presume that Layard and Jackman are not simply trying to exploit the partial relationship between inflation and the natural rate in the Phillips curve, which in any event, given the movement of actual unemployment in relation to the natural rate in this framework, is totally unclear, it appears that the authors are claiming that TIP both reduces the natural rate of unemployment, and also apparently—like the early US advocates of it—reduces cost-push inflation. It would be useful if Layard and Jackman would make explicit in future analysis precisely what they are claiming for TIP, and how the rate of monetary growth impinges on their analysis.

Inflationary measures to reduce long-term unemployment

On their proposals to reduce the duration of long-term unemployment, I do not have much to say. Having decided that benefits play little role, they have tried very hard to find imaginative projects for work that may have positive net marginal returns. In some ways I am reminded of Mundell's [1965] and Johnson's [1967] work on inflationary finance in less-developed countries (LDCs). You will recall that in this literature the authorities print money and use the proceeds to increase the capital stock. Even under the most favourable assumptions, for instance, a fixed capital to output ratio and no crowding-out of private investment, the resulting increase in growth and employment is arguably small in relation to the ensuing inflation (around 33 per cent on average inflation for a 1 per cent increase in the rate of growth). Layard and Jackman in effect suggest borrowing money to pay for their long-term unemployment measures. The precise effects of such policies will require a formal analysis which recognises the potential implications of their measures for expected future monetary growth and crowding-out, and includes all the possibilities on the supply side for employment substitution and the like. I would estimate that a lot of inflation might ultimately be created for very few jobs.

I would like to finish by raising one other point. In their model, firms set their prices as a mark-up on average cost. But the average cost of TIP itself is not included by them in firms' costs. Allowance for this factor can lead, under certain assumptions, to local instability of the economy (Peel [1979]).

REFERENCES

Johnson, H. G. [1967]: *Essays in Monetary Economics*, Allen and Unwin, London.

Layard, R. [1986]: *How to Beat Unemployment*, Oxford University Press, London.

Mundell, R. [1965]: 'Growth, Stability and Inflationary Finance', *Journal of Political Economy*.

Peel, D. A. [1979]: 'The Dynamic Behaviour of A Simple Macro Economic Model with a Tax Based Incomes Policy', *Economic Letters*.

Commentary—2
SAMUEL BRITTAN
Financial Times

Professor Layard is chairman of the Centre for Labour Economics, a highly academic institution. He is also chairman of the Charter for Jobs, which is—or would like to be—a campaigning organisation for the militant left-of-centre.

In his paper today with Richard Jackman and in his more comprehensive book *How to Beat Unemployment,*[1] on which I shall primarily focus, the two Professor Layards have both taken part; and it is important for the reader to try to distinguish between them. For the book contains many facts about unemployment which deserve to be better known, as well as a diagnosis which, if they understood it, would not be to the taste of some of those who might like to use the book as a campaign bible. Finally, the book contains a programme—most of which I would support on an emergency basis, but which I am not sure tackles the fundamental political economy of the subject.

Rise in long-term unemployment

The most outstanding feature of the rise in unemployment since 1980 is that the whole increase has been in long-term jobless, out of work for more than a year. The number unemployed for less has actually fallen. Transitional unemployment of two weeks or less is no higher than in 1975.

There has thus been little change in the number of people losing their jobs. But once someone has been on the register a while, his chances of finding a job are far, far worse than they used to be.

To use an analogy I first heard from Professor Alan Budd, flowers which are left over from the previous day have a double disadvantage: they are known to have been rejected and they are already one day old. The handicaps increase rapidly for older and older batches.

This concentration of unemployed among the long-term is also found in France, and to a certain extent in West Germany. On the

---

[1] Oxford University Press, London, 1986.

other hand, it is absent in economies as different as the USA and Sweden, in both of which only 12 per cent of the total jobless have been unemployed for more than a year. The total unemployment rate is also lower in Sweden and the USA.

Layard links these differences with the fact that social security is not open-ended in the last two countries. In the USA benefit runs out after six months, and in Sweden an unemployed person ceases to be eligible for benefit after 300 days if he has refused a place on a training or work programme.

But I would be extremely careful to avoid anything savouring of civilian conscription, for the sake of getting statistical unemployment totals down. Cures can be worse than the disease.

Unemployment is also highly concentrated among manual workers (who make up 84 per cent of unemployed men) and is also higher among young people. These discrepancies have always existed, but stand out more when the overall rate is high. There is here a contrast with West Germany, where youth pay is relatively less, but youth unemployment no higher than that of adults.

A less well-known fact is that only 50 per cent of the unemployed are married and only 19 per cent have two or more children. It is only the last group who might be as well or better off on the dole without earnings on the side. So the influence of social security is more indirect than commonly supposed.

Better known is the concentration of job losses in manufacturing. Manufacturing employment has fallen by 2 million since 1979, whilst services and other sectors have been roughly stable. The biggest percentage increase in unemployment has been in Northern Ireland, the North, the West Midlands and Wales—the West Midlands being a new entry to the black-spot regions.

Growth of labour force and unemployment

Layard has pretty conclusive evidence that unemployment has little to do with the size of the labour force. The labour force grew as rapidly in 1950-66 as in recent years, yet unemployment then was low and stable. In both the last two decades the Japanese—and still more the US—labour force grew more rapidly than the European one, but employment also grew much more.

So 'remedies' such as compulsory retirement, shorter hours, work-sharing and similar ones based on the lump-of-labour fallacy are likely to be as ineffective as they are defeatist. As Layard says, 'The one fatal heresy in economic analysis is to take output as given'. From this most populist errors flow.

The most novel fact Layard has unearthed is the growing discrepancy between vacancies and unemployment. The number of vacancies is as high or higher than in 1971, but male unemployment is four times as large. He attributes this discrepancy to workers becoming 'more choosy about taking such jobs as are available'. He ascribes this development not to benefit levels, but to the less strict application of the requirement that people on benefit should be genuinely looking for work.

A feasible real wage

Further diagnosis is more controversial. But Layard's research with Jackman and others suggests that at any one time there is a feasible real wage that the economy can deliver. Unemployment has to be high enough to make wage-bargainers settle for a target real wage equal to it. It is this target which determines the infamous NAIRU—the non-accelerating inflation rate of unemployment—or, if you like, the underlying rate.

If this is so, government action to restrain inflation is merely the mechanism by which real-wage objectives are brought in line with what the economy can afford. The root problem is excessive real-wage objectives; and to put the blame on restrictive government demand management—as Layard also tries very hard to do—is misplaced except for the odd year or two.

As 'the fundamental cause of unemployment is wage pressure' (Layard's words, not mine), union strength and union wage pressure aggravate unemployment. While union membership has been on a long-term decline in the USA there was an upward surge in most European countries in the late 1960s and 1970s.

> 'If Europe now has more employment problems than the USA, it is difficult to suppose that trends in union power have nothing to do with it.'

Layard does not resort to such cautious double negatives when criticising Mrs Thatcher's policies.

There has been a fall in the UK unionisation percentage in the 1980s, but a large part of this represents the decline of highly unionised sectors, above all manufacturing. There is also a disturbing econometric estimate suggesting that the 'union mark-up', that is the wage differential enjoyed by unionised workers over comparable non-unionised ones, has indeed been higher in the 1980s than in earlier years.

Layard insists that unemployment is caused not by 'too high real wages', but by aggressive 'real-wage behaviour'. The point is that employers determine real wages through the wage-price mark-up. With an unchanged mark-up, real-wage pressure may be translated directly into unemployment without real wages actually succeeding in rising. This is not a modification of the argument which need cause much loss of sleep to exponents of the pay-jobs link.

Inflationary critique

Layard should be read with most caution on 'aggregate demand'. His view that the Government has followed over-restrictive monetary and fiscal policies since 1979 holds water only if inflation is ignored. The Thatcher Government did not decide on election to bring about a doctrinal reduction in inflation. It was faced with a large jump in recorded inflation between 1978 and 1980, from 8 to 18 per cent. This reflected the second explosion in oil prices, its own unfortunate VAT increases, the collapse of pay policies, and much else. The decision it made was not to accommodate double-digit inflation by monetary and fiscal policies. If one is looking for blame, it is in the policies that allowed inflation to hit 18 per cent rather than in the refusal to accommodate that rate.

The general picture is that a combination of rising union power and easier benefit conditions brought the economy by the early 1980s to a position where any shock—whether due to oil, a rising exchange rate, or anything else—was met by business by the shedding of workers, some of whom joined the army of long-term unemployed, who were effectively out of the labour market.

Layard's own cure was fairly well known before this seminar, and it is set out in more detail in his paper with Jackman today. It consists basically of targeting increased demand on the long-term unemployed and other workers in excess supply, where the inflationary impact is likely to be modest. There would be a one-year job guarantee for those out of work for more than a year, through an expansion of the Community Programme, a special building improvement programme, and a £40-a-week per head subsidy to employers hiring long-term unemployed.

The skewing of employers' National Insurance contributions away from the lower-paid workers towards the more skilled, begun by Nigel Lawson in 1985 in the face of severe employer hostility, should be carried further, according to Layard. He believes that NIS should be removed altogether on net hirings in the depressed areas. And he also calls for a more flexible housing market without stating the politically unpopular truths on this subject. Of course he wants more education and training, as does Lord Young. And he cannot resist calling for more infrastructure spending, even though what is sensible in this call is already subsumed in his other proposals.

But the *pièce de résistance*, which provides the main mechanism for securing more jobs with no more inflation, is his well-known proposal for a severe tax on pay increases above a prescribed norm.

Many of the above proposals have been endorsed in my *Financial Times* columns, if only in desperation after seven years of ever-increasing unemployment. But I have two main objections.

Emergency measures, not long-term reforms

First, most of the measures are emergency ones, not long-term labour-market reforms. A tax on pay increases is feasible for one, two or perhaps three years, and it is better than a solemn and binding declaration from the TUC or statutory pay controls. But in the long run firms will take successful avoiding action, as they do over all forms of pay policy. Similarly, it is possible to subsidise marginal employment for a little while; but if the subsidies became permanent, companies would find means—even if it meant their own re-organisation—by which most of their workers became subsidy-worthy.

This is not to decry Layard's and Jackman's proposals. As both high and low unemployment feed on themselves, an emergency programme could have a long-lasting effect. But if not, more fundamental changes would be required. A possible link between the emergency programme and longer-term reforms is the exemption of genuinely profit-related pay increases from the pay tax.

My second reservation is more stratospheric. If a combination of a pay tax and selective unemployment measures can lead to more output and less inflation for any given growth of nominal demand, then the path projected in the 1986 Budget is generous enough.

Of course, if the Layard/Jackman programme were tried, so many economic relationships would change that further measures *might* be necessary to maintain nominal demand. But it is far from certain. And it was an unnecessary hostage to fortune to lay down a policy mix consisting of a fiscal boost combined with a high exchange rate, on which Layard understandably partially changed his mind while the book was going through the press. But while I know of better books on macro-economic policy, I do not know of a better one on British unemployment.

4. Curing Unemployment through Labour-Market Competition

MICHAEL BEENSTOCK
City University Business School

and

PATRICK MINFORD
University of Liverpool

With Commentaries by

JON SHIELDS
Employment Institute

The Authors

MICHAEL BEENSTOCK was born in 1946 and educated at the London School of Economics (BSc(Econ), 1967; MSc, 1968; PhD, 1976). He was Adviser, HM Treasury, 1970-76, on international monetary and energy problems; World Bank (Washington), 1976-78, on project appraisal and development planning; Senior Research Fellow, London Business School, 1978-81. Since 1981 he has been the Esmée Fairbairn Professor of Finance and Investment, City University Business School, and Director of the City Institute of Finance and Economic Review (CIFER).

He is author of *The Foreign Exchanges: Theory Modelling and Policy* (1978); *Health Migration and Development* (1980); *A Neo-classical Analysis of Macroeconomic Policy* (1980); *The World Economy in Transition* (1983); and *Insurance for Unemployment* (1986). For the IEA he has previously contributed papers, 'Fallacies in Counter-Inflation Policy', to its collection of essays entitled *Could Do Better* (Occasional Paper 'Special', No. 62, 1982), 'Social Policy for Social Democracy', to its symposium, *Agenda for Social Democracy* (Hobart Paperback No. 15, 1983), and '*The General Theory*, Secular Stagnation and the World Economy', to *Keynes's General Theory: Fifty Years On* (Hobart Paperback No. 24, 1986).

PATRICK MINFORD—see page 2.

I. INTRODUCTION

Persistently high unemployment is a manifestation of labour-market failure. A sustained and significant reduction in unemployment will be achieved only if fundamental reform of the labour market is undertaken. These reforms will transform a sclerotic labour market into a competitive one in which the laws of supply and demand are allowed to prevail. For it is when the laws of supply and demand do not operate that market imbalances are greatest; the labour market is no exception.

In the UK labour market the laws of supply and demand are severely inhibited in several respects. For example, attention has been drawn to the chronic state of the housing market which restricts labour mobility, especially for council-house tenants. British housing arrangements drastically reduce the incentive to 'get on your bike'. Attention has also been drawn to the influence of British social security arrangements on conditions in the labour market. Here, however, we focus on what we regard as the Achilles' tendon of the entire market: the way in which collective bargaining by trade unions prevents the price mechanism from operating and spawns a class of 'insiders'—members of unions that have successfully achieved relatively high rates of pay—and 'outsiders'—the unemployed or the low-paid.

Collective bargaining disenfranchises the unemployed of their market power to compete for the jobs of the unionised insiders. Moreover, in contrast to competitive wage bargaining, collective bargaining tends to generate unemployment and/or depressed non-union wage rates. Empirical evidence (below, pp. 135-138) shows that collective bargaining has the effect of raising wage rates, which in turn is likely to lead to unemployment. International patterns of unemployment, wage rates and unionisation reveal the contrast between the comparatively good unemployment record in the USA and the poor European record. The small and diminishing importance of US trade unions has been responsible for wage moderation and impressive employment growth at a time when the opposite constellation of events was happening in Europe.

We review recent developments in union power in Britain. Although highly militant behaviour has been checked, the underlying foundations of union powers in collective bargaining remain. This does not diminish the importance of what has been achieved, but it does mean that the basic malaise is still in place.

We show that various proposals such as 'profit-sharing' and 'tax-based incomes policies' are crude attempts at introducing wage flexibility and moderation designed to reduce unemployment. But these 'remedies' no more than tinker with a fundamentally flawed system of wage determination. They are to labour-market reform as milk quotas are to CAP reform—desperate attempts to live with a system that everyone knows to be sclerotic and socially unjust.

Instead, the sclerosis itself must be removed by fundamental reforms of the labour market which will replace collective bargaining by competitive bargaining. In practice, this amounts to the removal of the immunities and privileges that unions have traditionally enjoyed. Given the social concern about unemployment, this politically fraught conclusion is where the underlying forces of economic logic ultimately lead. If a market does not work, it should be made to do so for the sake of the unemployed.

II. COLLECTIVE BARGAINING AND LABOUR-MARKET SCLEROSIS

Figure 1 introduces our basic ideas without going into excessive detail; in it S and D denote labour supply and demand 'curves'. In a competitive labour market, supply and demand intersect at a and employment is L_c and the equilibrium wage W_c. If the labour market is unionised and wages are determined collectively rather than individually the wage rate is likely to be raised to W_u and employment is likely to fall to L_u. This occurs because, even in a democratic trade union, it may be shown[1] that there is likely to be a trade-off, such as curve II, in which different combinations of wages and employment give rise to equal levels of trade union utility. In Figure 1 utility is maximised at b if unions bargain only about wages, or it might be maximised at a point like c if they bargain about manning levels as well.[2] In either case employment is likely to suffer.

The basic insight behind this analysis is that a collective bargain

---

[1] A. Oswald, 'The Microeconomic Theory of the Trade Union', *Economic Journal*, September 1982.

[2] I. M. McDonald and R. M. Solow, 'Wage Bargaining and Employment', *American Economic Review*, December 1981.

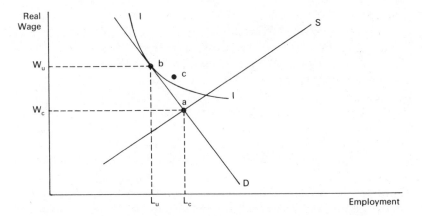

Figure 1: Collective Bargaining and Unemployment

which raises wages above competitive rates and reduces employment is a rational gamble. There is a probability that each member will be one of the lucky ones to survive the gamble and obtain more pay; but if he does not he will lose his job and either draw unemployment benefit or receive a lower non-union wage. The higher is the unemployment benefit rate, the more attractive the gamble and the higher will be the union wage.

Collective action and a 'chain reaction'

But collective action is likely to trigger a chain reaction in which wages are raised through a succession of bargaining rounds.[3] Suppose that collective action initially raises wages by 25 per cent above the competitive rate and a quarter of the workforce is laid off because the elasticity of demand for labour happens to be minus one, as various empirical studies suggest. The 75 per cent who survive the gamble will want to enter a second round to bargain for yet higher wages. They did not bargain for the higher wages in the first round because the survivors could not have known that they would be lucky and remain employed. But once they have survived, an incentive is established to try their luck again. They may be

---

[3] M. Beenstock, 'Regret and Jubilation in Union Wage Bargaining', City University Business School (mimeo), March 1987; *Oxford Economic Papers* (forthcoming).

restrained from this action by the original decision of those who gambled in the first round, and who would wish to protect themselves against successive gamblings by the most secure members. But there is no obvious mechanism to achieve such restraint.

If wages rise by another 10 per cent in the second round and employment falls by another 10 per cent, the survivors of the second round might then wish to entertain a third. Eventually the number of rounds converges because the cost and the risk of not surviving become increasingly large. But by the time the gamble is played out, the job losses will be a multiple of what they originally were.

The same logic gives rise to adverse ratchet-effects in which trade unions take advantage of benign developments to raise wages, but when these developments are reversed wages do not fall. These arguments imply that employment will tend to fall over time. For example, an autonomous increase in the demand for labour of 10 per cent, which gives unions an incentive to secure a 12 per cent wage increase, may in turn reduce union employment by 2 per cent. If the increase in labour demand is reversed, wages will fall by less than 12 per cent because 2 per cent of the membership have lost their say. So wages may only fall by perhaps 8 per cent, implying a total increase of 4 per cent and a total fall in employment of 4 per cent.

The dichotomy between 'insiders' and 'outsiders' in the labour market upon which this theory of sclerosis is based is being increasingly drawn upon by labour economists.[4] The various contributions to the literature differ in detail but they have one crucial thing in common. Trade unions by their collective action prevent equal access to employment opportunities. In particular, the unemployed outsiders have little or no market power. British labour-market institutions create a bias towards higher unemployment and make it very difficult for unemployment to be reduced once it has been increased.

---

[4] For example, A. Lindbeck and D. J. Snower, *Union Activity and Economic Resilience*, Discussion Paper No. 114, Centre for Economic Policy Research, June 1986; O. Blanchard and L. Summers, 'Hysteria and Unemployment', *European Economic Review*, 1986. The basis for all these theories is M. Olson, *The Logic of Collective Action*, Harvard University Press, 1965.

One of us[5] has investigated the effects on the losers of this gamble on wages and unemployment. The losers have willingly and rationally entered the succession of gambles; there has been free choice. But this was feasible in the first place only because unemployment benefit provided a safety net. Unemployment benefit creates moral hazards for collective wage bargains; it protects union members from some of the follies of their own actions. The losers have also disenfranchised themselves from the labour market; they cannot rejoin the game once they have lost. They have become outsiders while the surviving insiders have no incentive to reflect the interests of the new outsiders in the collective wage bargains they negotiate.

The policy implication of this analysis is that to reduce unemployment the unemployed must be re-enfranchised. They must be given the opportunity to compete for jobs in the unionised sector— their market power must be restored to them. There must be no dichotomy between insiders and outsiders, even if this result has been voluntarily produced (involuntarily in the case of new entrants to the labour market). This can be achieved only if the restrictive practice of collective bargaining is replaced by competitive bargaining. In terms of Figure 1 the abolition of collective bargaining is necessary if unemployment is to be reduced from b to a.

This argument does not imply that group behaviour as such must be made illegal. There is no harm in groups appointing representatives to bargain on their behalf. But the groups must not be provided with market powers that outsiders do not have. For example, they must be answerable for any damage that strike action might bring about, and they cannot exclude the employment of outsiders either as individuals or as groups. In this way the administrative advantages of group behaviour can be retained alongside the economic advantages of competition.

III. UNION MARK-UP

Thus far our discussion and proposals have been hypothetical. Does collective bargaining in practice raise wages above their competitive rates in the UK? It is the micro-economic evidence that is more likely to be reliable in this regard than its macro-economic

---

[5] M. Beenstock, *op. cit.*

counterpart because it deals with individual cases rather than large groups where averaging might obscure the truth. Table 1 summarises the main findings.

Empirical investigators generally agree that union wage-rates exceed those of their competitive counterparts, although the union mark-up in the UK appears to be smaller than in the USA. In the Table, estimates of the mark-up cluster around 10 per cent, although it appears that in the case of public-sector workers the mark-up may be considerably higher.

Figure 2 plots an estimate of the behaviour of the average mark-up over time; this series is not intended as a reliable measure of the actual mark-up, but rather as an indicator of its change over time. Over the period as a whole the mark-up has tended to rise. After substantial growth in the 1950s the mark-up accelerated between

TABLE 1

MICRO-ECONOMETRIC ESTIMATES
OF THE TRADE UNION MARK-UP IN BRITAIN

Study	Employment Type	Year of Study	Mark-up (%)
Stewart (1983)	Male manuals in manufacturing	1975	7.7
Shah (1984)	White manuals	1968-69	10.0
Layard, Metcalf & Nickell (1978)	Males	1973	25.0
Blanchflower (1986)	Manuals semi-skilled	1980	10.2
	Middle managers	1980	4.0
	Manuals semi-skilled manufacturing	1980	14.0
	Manuals semi-skilled public sector	1980	25.5
	Public sector clerical	1980	12.4

Sources: M. B. Stewart, 'Relative Earnings and Individual Union Membership in the UK', *Economica*, May 1983.
A. Shah, 'Job Attributes and the Size of the Union–Non-Union Wage Differential', *Economica*, November 1984.
R. Layard, D. Metcalf and S. Nickell, 'The Effects of Collective Bargaining on Relative and Absolute Wages', *British Journal of Industrial Relations*, 1978, pp. 287-302.
D. Blanchflower, 'What Effects do Unions have on Relative Wages in Great Britain?', *British Journal of Industrial Relations*, July 1986.

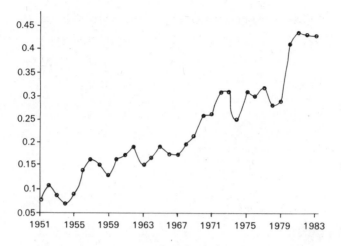

Figure 2: The Union Mark-up for Male Manual Workers, 1951-83

Source: Supplied by R. Layard and S. Nickell, based upon Layard, Metcalf and Nickell [1978], *op. cit.* (Table 1).

1968 and 1972 before jumping again in 1977-81. If indeed the data represent a measure of union power, what are the factors that have generated it? Here we explore the following hypotheses:

(i) That union power varies directly with the real rates of unemployment benefit because, as discussed above, collective action becomes more attractive when the effects of job losses become less onerous.

(ii) That the mark-up varies directly with the proportion of the workforce that is unionised. Does union power then vary disproportionately with union density since strength might lie in unity?

(iii) That the mark-up is cyclical; in particular, that unions are better at protecting their wage-rates during recessions than their non-union counterparts—i.e., non-union wages are relatively more flexible. Similar considerations apply to inflation, where unions night be better at protecting members' wages from inflation and slow to react when inflation falls.

(iv) That the mark-up is temporarily held in check during bouts of incomes policy since at these times union muscle cannot be exercised.

Testing Hypotheses about the Union Mark-up

The data in Figure 2 are explained by the following multiple regression model:[6]

$$UMU = -0.41 + 1.17\hat{U} + 1.38\ BEN + 0.49\ \dot{U}D + 0.04\ GOV$$
$$\quad\quad (6.2)\ (3.9)\quad (7.2)\quad\quad (3.5)\quad\quad (3.3)$$

$\bar{R}^2 = 0.94$ $= 0.026$ $DW = 1.8$

where

UMU = percentage union mark-up
U   = rate of unemployment
BEN = real value of Supplementary Benefits
UD = union density
GOV = government dichotomy variable (1 = Tory, 0 = Labour)
( ) = 't' value

(v)   That the mark-up depends on which government is in office. Here there are two possibilities: that the unions co-operate with Labour, or that they take advantage of Labour and are constrained by the Conservatives.

The Box shows the results of testing these hypotheses. They suggest that the mark-up is anti-cyclical since it varies directly with the rate of unemployment, it varies directly with the real value of benefits and union density, and it tends to be 4 per cent higher under Tory governments than Labour governments. Incomes policy did not appear to affect the mark-up, nor did inflation. The equation draws attention to the fact that, among other factors, social security benefits tend to enhance trade-union power and the incentives for anti-social collective action.

IV.   THE SOURCE OF UNION POWER IN BRITAIN

That unions are still, in spite of the laws brought in by Mr Norman Tebbit, powerful in Britain in wage negotiations cannot be denied. The union mark-up, as measured in Figure 2, still shows no fall

---

[6] C. Whitbread and M. Beenstock, 'Explaining the Union Mark-up in Britain 1951-1983', City University Business School (mimeo), December 1986.

from its 1980 level; it had increased steadily over the previous three decades. The plateau since 1980 indicates at best an arresting of union power over wages.

Why have the laws not dented this particular power? There is a general perception that unions are now 'weak'; and this is certainly true in negotiations over redundancies and working practices where they have been largely powerless to stop massive change, as evidenced by the surge in productivity in manufacturing since 1979 and also more anecdotally in service sectors—such as printing and cleaning—where good productivity statistics are harder to come by.

The legislation nonetheless preserves immunity for action on pay and conditions which is backed by the workers. Any attempt by management to cut union wages could well provoke a strike of this sort. But making workers redundant while increasing the wages of the majority for more productive working practices is a different matter. First, the majority of workers benefit and so will not back a strike. Second, a strike on such a matter may well not attract legal immunity, for it is not strictly about 'pay and conditions', and redundancies made within the law (with due notice and redundancy pay) are probably not in this category. Third, many firms have offered attractive redundancy terms, and successfully asked for voluntary redundancies, so in many cases even workers made redundant would not oppose.

Increased efficiency, fewer jobs

The main measures have therefore much increased efficiency in the use of employer resources but they have not, as was hoped from a more general limitation of union power, created jobs at these higher levels of efficiency, by also reducing union wages. Rather, the increase in efficiency has, on balance, and certainly in the short run, *reduced* jobs. This situation is to be contrasted with the USA, for example, where weak unions have agreed to large 'give-backs'— reductions of wages in return for lower redundancies.

These results were not intended in the original conception of union reform. But in retrospect it was inevitable they would come about if the new laws were to be accepted by the bulk of union members, many of whom voted Conservative in 1979 and 1983. For these people would not be likely to accept reductions in living standards for the sake of increased job opportunities among the unemployed; true, society would be better off because the unemployed would be producing and so would not be a burden on the tax-payer, but a mechanism for re-distributing this gain to union members was not legitimate and was certainly not in existence.

The main hopes for jobs from union reform must in these circumstances be the faster growth of non-union firms, permitted by the restraints on the closed shop and on union secondary action (often used in the past to 'black' non-union suppliers). This is, unfortunately, a much slower process of job creation and erosion of union effects on aggregate wages than the direct path of union wage cuts. But there is some tentative evidence of progress in the expansion of self-employment (up by 39 per cent since 1979) and of small firms (up by 10 per cent since 1979) and in the fall in union membership since 1980 (Table 4).

If this diagnosis is accepted, it follows that the Conservative reforms suffer from a crucial lacuna: they left the immunities intact in the very area where unions affect job *creation*. They were effective enough where unions affect *productivity* through over-manning. They therefore triggered off job-shedding on a massive scale, without the corresponding falls in wages that would have expanded jobs elsewhere and so at least partly offset this job-shedding.

We will suggest in our last section how policy could now react to this lacuna. But before leaving the question of union power, we should clear up some theoretical issues as applied to Britain. The union model used in this paper assumes that unions push up wages in sectors where they have power and that they also push for other aspects of their job conditions package—such as slower work rates, demarcation, job security, improved work environment; the model is in essentials a monopoly model, where unions 'set' a price/quality and firms then react to this by fixing quantity of labour hired. According to this model, union power over one part of the package (work rates, etc.) was drastically reduced by the Tebbit laws, and firms were able to react by reducing the quantity of labour.

An alternative model of bilateral monopoly (between a union and a firm or industry) has it that the parties reach an optimal bargain which fixes employment so as to maximise their joint gains at the expense of the firms' customers but which fixes wages as well. This argument does not, however, fit the facts of the UK where employment has now collapsed. It should not have been affected by reduced union power; rather, wages should have fallen as the share-out changed in favour of firms.

Yet another model has been suggested by Professors Freeman and Medoff[7] and their colleagues at Harvard. According to this, management slack in firms is reduced by unions using their power; they force arrangements to raise productivity in order to satisfy unions' demands. Again, this model does not fit UK experience. It has been the reduction of union power that has raised productivity by reducing restrictive union practices.

The institutional structure of the UK labour market, with large unions dealing across numerous firms in a wide variety of products and labour types, supports the traditional monopoly model we have used here against the bilateral model described above. The transaction costs of bilateral bargaining would be prohibitive. The high degree of competition in most *product* markets, because of British openness in trade and the abolition of resale price maintenance, also militates against the Freeman-Medoff model of x-inefficiency.

In short, there seems every reason to use the union monopoly model to analyse UK experience; and according to that model, unions still exercise considerable power over wages, to the detriment of jobs.

V. THE 'EUROPEAN DISEASE'

We have drawn attention to the interdependence between trade union power, the social security system and unemployment in the UK. Here we draw attention to the fact that this unhealthy synergy has been largely responsible for the growth in unemployment elsewhere in Europe. How does the 'European Disease' compare with the relatively clean bill of health that prevails in the United States?

Labour-market institutions differ across European countries, making it difficult to use a common model. It is quite inappropriate to attempt to replicate results estimated for the UK in other countries without careful consideration of their respective national

---

[7] R. B. Freeman and J. L. Medoff, *What do Unions do?*, Basic Books, New York, 1984.

labour-market institutions. One of us has been involved[8] in a study of developments in the Belgian and West German labour markets, drawing upon the broad theoretical ideas to which reference has already been made. On the whole, when allowance is made for institutional differences, the evidence from Belgium and West Germany is qualitatively similar to that from the UK.

Table 2 reports the long-run effects of increases in benefit and increased unionisation for the three countries. In the UK a 1 per cent increase in benefits raises wages by 0.48 per cent (possibly partly via the extra union power that is promoted). In Germany and Belgium wages rise by 0.85 per cent and 0.29 per cent respectively. In the UK a 1 percentage point increase in union density raises wages by 1.6 per cent whereas in Germany and Belgium the increases are estimated at a substantial 10 and 0.8 per cent respectively. These wage responses bring about the unemployment responses reported in Table 2 when allowance is made for the return effect of unemployment upon wages.

Changes in union power brought about by more generous social security provision and the spread of union membership, together with the direct consequences of higher benefits and tax rates, have raised the equilibrium rate of unemployment in the three countries, as indicated in Table 3. Since 1973 the more generous social security policies of the SPD in Germany have substantially increased the rate of unemployment, while in Belgium these effects were concentrated between 1970 and 1975. The increase in unemployment in West Germany and Belgium on account of the effects that we identify has been proportionately larger than in the UK.

TABLE 2

THE LONG-RUN EFFECTS OF UNION POWER
ON UNEMPLOYMENT IN EUROPE

per cent

	UK	Germany	Belgium
10 per cent rise in benefits	26	15	16
1 percentage point rise in union density	9	20	4

[8] J. Davis and P. Minford, 'Germany and the European Disease', *Recherches Économiques de Louvain*, 1986.

TABLE 3
THE ESTIMATED EQUILIBRIUM RATE OF UNEMPLOYMENT IN THREE EUROPEAN COUNTRIES, 1965 TO 1983

	UK	*W. Germany*	*Belgium*
1965	500,000	200,000	30,000
1970	2,000,000	220,000	40,000
1975	1,200,000	590,000	315,000
1980	2,500,000	1,050,000	340,000
1983	2,000,000	1,250,000	n.a.

VI.   USA *v* EUROPE—A CASE STUDY

Figure 3 records the remarkable contrast between the employment records of Europe and North America over the last 10 years. In Europe the numbers in employment have remained more or less static while in North America employment has grown at an average rate of a little over 2 per cent per annum, or more than twice as fast as Japanese employment growth. During 1980-82 North American

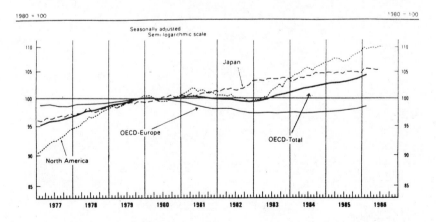

Figure 3:   Employment in Various Parts of the World, 1977-86

Source: OECD Main Economic Indicators.

143

employment stabilised, reflecting the recession after the second OPEC price rise; in contrast, European employment fell during this period.

Some commentators have remarked that the impressive North American record coincided with the increase in the US budget deficit in the early 1980s and that it is essentially a Keynesian phenomenon. The flaw in this thesis is that the dynamism of US employment goes back well before this date. Others have noted that the relative dynamism of US employment and the dismal European record reflects the behaviour of real wages, which has been moderate in the US and immoderate in Europe. Figure 4 plots various US and European real-wage indices which testify to the remarkable degree of real-wage moderation in the USA, and the equally remarkable lack of moderation in Europe. Real-wage differences go a long way to explain the relative employment performance of North America and Europe.

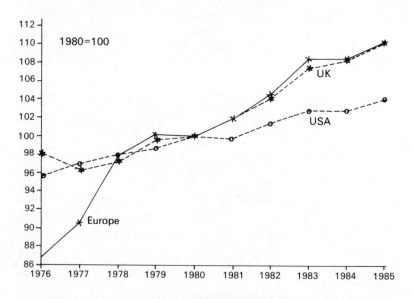

Figure 4: Own-Product Real Wages, 1976-85

Sources: US: business sector, *Monthly Labour Review*.
Europe: manufacturing, OECD Main Economic Indicators.
UK: average earnings deflated by GDP deflator, *Blue Book*.

But this begs the question: Why did real wages behave so differently on either side of the Atlantic? Our thesis is that the US labour market is more flexible and competitive than its sclerotic European counterpart. Labour-market competition has kept US real wages in check, while the lack of competition in Europe has allowed them to drift upwards and has caused them to fail to respond to demographic as well as oil price shocks. The inflexibility in Europe reflects the high degree of unionisation, while the flexibility in the US reflects the low and declining rates of unionisation. This insight leads us to conclude that, if US labour-market institutions were adopted in Europe, the lacklustre European employment record would be radically transformed.

Table 4 records union densities for the USA and three European countries. A striking feature of the Table is the historically low degree of unionisation in the USA. Equally important in the present context is the declining role of US trade unions. It is conceivable that falling union density is induced by changes in the nature of economic activity and where it is produced rather than autonomous declines in membership. Between 1961 and 1984, however, Doyle[9] attributes more than half of the decline to autonomous forces: US workers have increasingly been preferring to be non-unionists.

But there is also much to be learnt from the induced fall in union

TABLE 4

PROPORTION OF WORKERS BELONGING TO TRADE UNIONS, 1960–84

per cent

	USA*	W. Germany	Belgium	UK
1960	31.4	37.2	62.0	43.1
1965	28.4	36.0	63.0	43.2
1970	27.0	35.8	68.9	50.9
1975	24.5	39.2	75.8	53.7
1980	25.2	40.3	77.3	56.4
1984	18.8	41.5	n.a.	53.9

*Excludes agricultural workers and includes the unemployed in the denominator.

---

[9] P. M. Doyle, 'Area Wage Surveys Shed Light on Declines in Unionisation', *Monthly Labour Review*, September 1985.

membership. Over the period 1973-85, Rones[10] (Figure 5) shows that there has been a marked shift of US employment from the 'snowbelt' to the 'sunbelt'. Union representation has traditionally been higher in the northern states, and Olson[11] as well as Hulten and Schwab[12] attribute this contrast not only to the lower union presence in the 'sunbelt' but also to the lack of producers' vested interests there. In short, the dynamism of US employment has, by and large, been concentrated outside the union sector. This, in turn, has forced the residual union sector to adapt or die: the threat of relocation of business has necessitated a degree of flexibility that is absent in an economy where there is less scope for regional

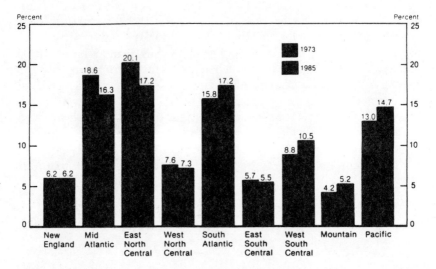

Figure 5: The Drift of Non-agricultural Employment from the Unionised Snowbelt to the Non-unionised Sunbelt in the USA, 1973-85

Source: Rones, *op. cit.*, percentage shares of employment.

[10] P. L. Rones, 'An Analysis of Regional Employment Growth 1973-1985', *Monthly Labour Review*, July 1986.

[11] M. Olson, 'The South Will Fall Again: the South as Leader and Laggard in Economic Growth', *Southern Economic Journal*, April 1983.

[12] C. R. Hulten and R. M. Schwab, 'Regional Productivity and the Growth in US Manufacturing 1951-1978', *American Economic Review*, March 1984.

TABLE 5
RATIO OF UNION TO NON-UNION WAGES IN USA, 1984-86 (1981 Q2 = 100)

		Total	*Manufacturing*	*Non-manufacturing*
1984	Q1	101.2	100.6	102.5
	2	101.0	100.5	102.0
	3	100.8	100.5	101.8
	4	100.4	100.0	101.2
1985	Q1	99.7	99.1	100.4
	2	99.7	99.1	100.4
	3	99.1	99.2	99.5
	4	99.0	99.1	99.4
1986	Q1	98.7	98.4	99.2

Source: *Monthly Labour Review*, August 1986.

competition. Indeed, union wage-rates have, on the whole, been as moderate as those of their non-union counterparts (Table 5).

VII. THE POLICY RESPONSE

Britain suffers from an obvious lack of competition for jobs over which unions have control through wage-setting. The size of this union sector has shrunk, as unions have lost their power to maintain restrictive practices; but like an Armada shorn of a few outlying frigates, it has closed ranks and cruised on. Firms in this sector are unable to appoint non-union labour at low wage-rates, and since the sector is large and powerful, non-union firms can make only slow and limited headway over these large areas of our economy.

There is no lack of proposals to replace current British labour-market institutions with new ones: various incomes policies or new tribunals (suggested, for example, by Professor James Meade) would command unions and firms to fix certain wages or face various penalties. One problem with these proposals is that they fly in the face of British traditions of economic freedom; they also entail bureaucracy and, because the rules can never be flexible enough to accommodate the requirements of particular firms or sectors, they create inter-firm and inter-sectoral distortions, often penalising the most enterprising and the fastest-growing.

The 'blunderbuss' of TIP

Tax-based incomes policy (TIP) is supposedly different: excessive wage increases would be taxed, with the proceeds returned to industry in lump-sum transfers.[13] The tax would be a permanent new feature of our system, designed to penalise firms and sectors where real wages were rising fastest. But as a weapon to *reduce* the union mark-up it is woefully inadequate; for, as shown in Figure 2 (above, p. 137), the mark-up is on a plateau and to stay there real wages must have risen at the same rate as elsewhere! What the tax would do is create severe distortions penalising growing firms, the last thing the British economy requires. It would also, like all the other incomes policies, create a new bureaucracy. Thus TIP is like a blunderbuss, poor in aim and destructive in impact.

Another example of tinkering is found in profit-sharing schemes (PSS), which give employees a basic wage plus an element related to profits. The latter rises in booms and falls in slumps so that effective real wages will be stabilised, which will help in turn to stabilise employment. PSS, too, must be regarded as a backdoor way of reducing the control that trade unions have over wages. In a slump they would forfeit their ability to preserve their members' real wages and in this way employment would be stabilised. Trade union leaders have, however, seen through the veil of PSS and have rejected the idea since it diminishes their power.

Tinkering will not work. A spade must be called a spade. Only direct reform will work if it is politically feasible; nothing will work if it is not. The basic issue lies in union power and collective bargaining.

Legal reform the only durable solution

We seek solutions which preserve economic freedom under the law and which do not incur unnecessary costs in bureaucracy and distortion. The obvious route to take, therefore, is a legal one.

British trade unions have been dangerously powerful bodies essentially since the 1906 Act which gave them immunity from tort actions (for inducement to breach of contract). It was the retraction of that immunity that reduced their power to obstruct rises in productivity. The obvious next step should be to remove all

---

[13] *cf.* Jackman and Layard, above, pp. 104–107.

remaining immunities from the processes of the common law; why should any economic agent, individual or group, be above the law? For this is what the 1906 Act achieved for unions; since Parliament is sovereign, it was able to override the natural justice evolved under the common law.

With immunity gone, unions would be compelled to negotiate contracts. These contracts would specify the conditions under which a strike would be legal. Presumably, for example, it would be legal if the employer broke the contract in certain ways; and on the expiry of a wage agreement, during the run-up to a new agreement, it might also be legal. Who knows what individual firms would agree to? But the point is that the law of contract would once again prevail in industrial relations.

But this reform alone would probably not be enough. Many firms would prefer a quiet life with the unions they know (and love?). The recent experience of Fleet Street shows it is the intervention of an 'outside' competitor, and not a quiet life, that creates movement. So the brief of the Monopolies Commission must be extended in practice to examine conditions where non-union entry into an industry is prevented directly or indirectly by unions or union-dominated firms. The Act setting the Commission up permits this extension. But it has not been used.

We have argued this case in detail before—it is not a new proposal.[14] The Government went ahead in sympathy with much of those earlier arguments and produced a series of labour laws in a step-by-step procedure. The logic of their earlier action leads to further steps towards implementation of the full proposal, since manifestly the earlier action has left a major and highly damaging aspect of union power largely intact.

---

[14] E.g., P. Minford (with P. Ashton, D. Davies, M. Peel and A. Sprague), *Unemployment—Cause and Cure*, Basil Blackwell, Oxford, 2nd edn. 1985.

Commentary

JON SHIELDS

Employment Institute

This paper reads like two papers rather than one. One paper is inspired polemic. It trumpets the case for atomistic markets and thus justifies on simple *a priori* grounds a further erosion of trade-union immunities and effective extension of Monopolies Commission activities into trade-union behaviour. The second paper is a display of econometric estimates about the size and effects (but not causes) of trade-union power as revealed in the excess of union over non-union wages. Nowhere is there an attempt to link the two by articulating, let alone quantifying, the specific effects on wages of the legal immunities of unions or preclusion of entry into an industry by firms using non-union labour.

This lack of a real empirical base for the paper is highlighted by its failure to address some basic facts about unemployment and trade-union activity in recent years.

First, unemployment. On present definitions, adult unemployment rose from a local peak of 850,000 in 1972 to 1.3 million in 1977, declined a bit for a couple of years and then rose dramatically from 1.2 million in 1979 to 3.1 million in 1986. The fundamental economic phenomenon of the 1980s in Britain is mass unemployment.

Second, union power. Here, measurement is much more difficult. But there seems little reason to doubt recent ministerial claims that activity and power are at their lowest levels for decades. Working days lost through stoppages are likely to be below 2 million this year, compared with an average of about 10 million days a year lost through the 1970s. The number of new stoppages in 1986 is estimated at well under 1,000, making the average for the 1980s about 1,200 stoppages per year—less than half the frequency measured in the 1970s.

'Uphill struggle'

Against this background, two economists who seek to establish that the most effective route to lower unemployment is through a reduction in trade-union power are facing an uphill struggle.

Undaunted by the likelihood that recent macro-economic policy is the most likely explanation of current levels of unemployment—and the most powerful weapon to reverse the situation—they resort to international examples and model simulations to demonstrate the potential impact of making unions less powerful.

The problem with the type of international examples presented in the paper is that you can prove anything if you are selective enough. The United States is presented as a case study of how well an industrial country can do if unions are forced into retreat (although we are also told that remaining mark-ups are high). It is asserted that the long-run dynamism of employment growth in the United States belies the Keynesian interpretation of its recent impressive record on unemployment compared with Europe. But the paper admits (Figure 3) that growth of employment stagnated in North America from 1979 to 1982. Since 1982, employment growth has been so buoyant that it has not only absorbed the trend rise in labour supply but also caused an enormous inroad into US unemployment. This is fully consistent with a 'Keynesian' explanation, which blames the effects of tight monetary policy (on top of OPEC's second big price rise) for the severe recession followed by an expansionary fiscal policy generating a recovery.

There are, of course, other countries that could have been considered in an overview of where unemployment has been successfully held at bay. Sweden, Austria, Norway and Switzerland easily come to mind. Admittedly, union density is rather low in Switzerland. But no one could make this claim of Sweden, Austria and Norway. They all have unionisation rates some way above our own. Yet *none* of them has seen unemployment rates much above 4 per cent for decades. Clearly, *their* models of union involvement do not work at the expense of employment.

It would have been instructive to see some acknowledgement of this situation in the paper or some attempt to grapple with the reasons for the success of such countries. A possibility is, for instance, that centralised unions can actually have a very positive role to play in economic adjustment, particularly where there is a history of involvement and consensus in economic management.

Corporatist labour-market responses

To help systematic analysis in this area, Bruno and Sachs [1985] have established a ranking of industrialised countries by their degree of corporatism. Corporatist labour markets are those where national negotiations predominate over local ones; employers co-ordinate their moves and local labour organisations and shop stewards have limited power relative to the centre.

Dr Charles Bean, of the Centre for Labour Economics (in Bean *et al.* [1986]), has investigated whether a country's corporatist ranking affects the estimated response of wages or unemployment to external shocks. It does. In general, the more corporatist an economy, the larger the estimated response of wages to unemploy-ment—particularly in the short run—and the quicker the whole adjustment of the labour market to shocks.

It is, of course, true that some countries exhibiting a high degree of corporatism also have high unemployment (such as Belgium or the Netherlands). Corporatism will not necessarily bring about the sort of long-run changes in real wages and hence unemployment that Beenstock and Minford want. But the results suggest that a different policy route from legislation or a new Monopolies Com-mission could be pursued even if one accepted the authors' asser-tions about the effects of union power in the UK.

The union mark-up

As far as actual empirical evidence is concerned, we are provided in the paper with estimates of the size and behaviour of the union mark-up in the UK, possible determinants of it, and the estimated impact of the mark-up on equilibrium unemployment. On the implausibility of the latter estimates I shall venture only one thought: the disparity between observed unemployment and figures for so-called equilibrium—that is, explained—unemployment must surely render the estimates meaningless—other than as expository arithmetical indicators of the properties of the models themselves. It cannot be a good advertisement for the economics profession for such estimates to be presented as if they were genuine features of the real world. On the size of the union mark-up, I was pleased to see the authors give rather more weight to estimates in the range of 7-10 per cent than the much larger numbers that have sometimes been claimed. It was also good to see some innovative estimates of the determinants of the mark-up.

Much more difficult is to have any confidence in the displayed results. We are asked to believe that an equation for the mark-up deploying only contemporaneous variables and including such endogenous factors as unemployment levels and union density displayed no problems with dynamics or simultaneity. We are not given any clues to the dimensions of the variables, but it is tempting to believe that the unavoidable spikiness of the annualised data could be the main explanation of the equation's revealed associations of the mark-up with the electoral cycle—both through the government variable and the value of Supplementary Benefits. Whatever the merit of this equation, it is perfectly consistent with the contention that the mark-up has recently been kept at a high number primarily by the depth of the recession. Contrary to the assertions of the paper, the underlying bargaining power of unions over wages may actually have been substantially eroded in recent years, but the impact on the mark-up has simply been obscured by the direct effects of high unemployment.

Summing up

Much of this paper is preoccupied with a one-sided view of the labour market. Collusive or monopolistic employers come into the picture only to be rejected as unimportant because they have not succeeded in reducing real wages under high unemployment. Multi-occupation, multi-industry unions in the private sector seem to rule the roost, only occasionally troubled by unemployment or the arrival of a Labour Government.

The truth would have to acknowledge the justifiable defensive role which many unions play. It would also have to recognise that the main characteristic of an 'insider' is not that he or she is a union member, but simply that he is in work. The real outsiders remain the long-term unemployed. That is why proposals aimed directly at reducing wage pressure or providing guaranteed jobs for the long-term unemployed offer much more hope for the unemployed than further constraints on trade unions. To misattribute a quote from Beenstock and Minford, such action 'seems rather like a blunderbuss, poor in aim and destructive in impact'.

REFERENCES

Bruno, M. and J. Sachs, *The Economics of Worldwide Stagflation* [1985]: Basil Blackwell, Oxford.

Bean, C. R., P. R. G. Layard and S. J. N. Nickell, *The Rise in Unemployment: A Multi-Country Study* [1986]: Discussion Paper No. 239, Centre for Labour Economics, London.

The Commentary Authors

Alan Budd has been Williams and Glyn's Research Fellow in Banking, London Graduate School of Business Studies, since 1974; now Professor of Economics. Universities of Southampton, 1966–69, and Carnegie-Mellon, 1969–70. Senior Economic Adviser, Treasury, 1970–74. Editor, *Economic Outlook*; author of *The Politics of Economic Planning* (1978). For the IEA, he contributed a paper, 'Disarming the Treasury', to the Seminar, *The Taming of Government* (IEA Readings No. 21, 1979), and an essay, 'On Keynesian Unemployment and the Unemployment of Keynes', to the symposium on *Keynes's* General Theory: *Fifty Years On* (Hobart Paperback No. 24, 1986).

David Currie is Professor at Queen Mary College, University of London, and Director of the Research Programme in International Macro-economics at the Centre for Economic Policy Research. He was recently Houblon-Norman Fellow at the Bank of England and currently holds a post at the National Institute of Economic and Social Research. His most recent publications have been in monetary and international macro-economics.

Charles Goodhart is the Norman Sosnow Professor of Banking and Finance at the London School of Economics. For 17 years he was monetary economist at the Bank of England, becoming its Chief Adviser in 1980. Fellow of Trinity College, Cambridge, an Adviser to the Department of Economic Affairs and a Lecturer in Economics at the LSE. Author of books and articles on monetary issues, both analytical and empirical. He is currently completing a textbook, *Money, Information and Uncertainty,* on contemporary monetary economics.

Harold Rose is Esmée Fairbairn Visiting Professor of Finance, London Graduate School of Business Studies, and Group Economic Adviser to Barclays Bank since 1975. He was educated at Davenant Foundations School and the London School of Economics and Political Science. Head of the Economic Intelligence Department of the Prudential Assurance Company, 1948–58. Director of Studies to the Course in Industrial Financing, London

School of Economics, 1958–63; Reader in Economics, University of London, 1963–65; Esmée Fairbairn Professor of Finance, London Graduate School of Business Studies, 1965–75. Author of *The Economic Background to Investment* (1960); *Management Education in the 1970s: Growth and Issues* (1969). For the IEA he wrote *Disclosure in Company Accounts* (Eaton Paper 1, 1963, second edition, 1965) and a Commentary to *Choice in Currency* (Occasional Paper 48, 1976). He is a Trustee of the IEA.

David Peel is Professor of Economics at the University College of Wales, Aberystwyth. Formerly Senior Lecturer and then Reader in Economics at Liverpool University. He has written numerous articles on macro-economics and is co-author of *Rational Expectations and the New Macro Economics, Introduction to Economic Models of the UK, Expectations: Theory and Evidence*, and *Economics of Wage Control*.

Samuel Brittan was educated at Kilburn Grammar School and Jesus College, Cambridge, where he took First-Class Honours in Economics. He then held various posts on the *Financial Times* (1955–61); was Economics Editor of the *Observer* (1961–64); an Adviser at the Department of Economic Affairs (1965); and has been principal economic commentator on the *Financial Times* since 1966 and Assistant Editor since 1978. Member of the Peacock Committee on the financing of the BBC. Author of numerous books, of which the most recent is *The Role and Limits of Government* (1983). For the IEA he has written *Government and the Market Economy* (Hobart Paperback 2, 1971), *Participation without Politics* (Hobart Paper 62, 1975, 2nd edn., 1979), *How to End the 'Monetarist' Controversy* (Hobart Paper 90, 1981, 2nd edn., 1982), and his Wincott Memorial Lecture, *Two Cheers for Self-interest* (Occasional Paper 73, 1985).

Jon Shields has been Director of the Employment Institute and its associate Charter for Jobs since their formation in 1985. He was educated at Manchester Grammar School, Imperial College, London, and Churchill College, Cambridge. He was formerly senior economic adviser to the Treasury reponsible for international monetary institutions, and an economic adviser to the DHSS. He is co-editor of *Economic Report* (Charter for Jobs).